CREATE ONLINE

AND

GROW RICH

HOW YOU CAN ESCAPE THE 9 TO 5,
HAVE TIME FREEDOM, AND
DO WHAT YOU LOVE

ELKE CLARKE

CREATE ONLINE AND GROW RICH
www.CreateOnlineAndGrowRich.com

Publisher
10-10-10 Publishing
Markham, ON
Canada

Printed in Canada and the United States of America

CONTENTS

Praise for

Create Online and Grow Rich

"Elke's passion to help and inspire creative designers to do what they love and be profitable online shines through in this book. Her expertise in digital content, online marketing, and branding is why she is successful on Zazzle, year after year. Elke is an international authority on how to sell effectively on Zazzle, and has helped other Zazzle designers become successful with her proven plan. Elke Clarke's book, *Create Online and Grow Rich*, will inspire you, motivate you, and guide you to start on your own Zazzle journey to success."

– Diana Adair
Former Director of Communications at Zazzle

"Elke is *the real deal* when it comes to making money online. Her effective use of SEO and online marketing strategies to grow and maintain her 7-figure business in an ever-changing online space, makes her the go-to authority for every creative wanting to make money doing what they love. Elke Clarke's book, *Create Online and Grow Rich,* provides you with the perfect solution and proven plan to create a profitable online business, using your creativity."

– Martin Shervington
Marketing Strategist, International Speaker
Founder, Plus Your Business
Former Google SMB Advisor

"If you want to turn your creativity into substantial online income so that you can have the life you always dreamed of, then this book is a must-buy. *Create Online and Grow Rich* is the ultimate road map, full of marketing and business strategies, and success stories of how to make money online."

– James MacNeil
International Speaker, Bestselling Author and Founder of *Verbal Aikido* and *Pure Spiritual Intelligence*

"Create Online and Grow Rich should be mandatory reading for every free soul creative who wants to turn their art, photography and graphic designs into income, so that they can do what they love full-time, while earning a passive online   income."

Katalin Bátor-Hős,
Artist, Author, Creative Mindset Spark
Member of The 5 Step Profit Plan VIP Mentoring Program™

"Create Online and Grow Rich is a must-read for artists and digital creatives who want to learn the foundational principals for achieving the joy and financial freedom that comes from having a successful online passive income business."

Kate Thompson
Artist and Owner at Cedar and String
Member of The 5 Step Profit Plan VIP Mentoring Program™

"Take a big step forward in turning your dream of making money online with your creativity into reality with Elke Clarke. Elke is an expert in teaching how you can create and sell online faster and easier than you thought possible! Her advice and tips have been life-changing for me."

Shabnam Ahsan
Blogger, Graphic Designer and Online Entrepreneur
Member of The 5 Step Profit Plan VIP Mentoring
Program™

"Elke Clarke is the real deal. It is no exaggeration to say The 5 Step Profit Plan has transformed my business and my life. With Elke's structured plan and mentoring, I am building a profitable business part time from home, allowing me to care for my disabled husband. This book is a must read and then sign up for her program as soon as possible. I couldn't have done it without Elke and The 5 Step Profit Plan."

Rebecca Lewis
Artist, Owner of Bex Cottage Studio
Member of The 5 Step Profit Plan VIP Mentoring
Program™

I dedicate this book to you, the digital creative entrepreneur. Live your dream life doing what you love by creating online and growing rich.

Acknowledgments

Thank you to my three children, who are my "Why". I am blessed to have you in my life and am proud that each of you are following your dreams.

Thank you to my family and friends for supporting me through my extraordinary journey in life so far. I know you will always be there for me as my future unfolds with more extraordinary adventures.

Thank you to my publisher and mentor, Raymond Aaron, at 10-10-10 Publishing. It's been a pleasure and honor. I look forward to exploring more opportunities with you in the future.

Thank you to all of my amazing members in The 5 Step Profit Plan VIP Mentoring Program™. I am proud of your accomplishments and am privileged to be your mentor on your journey to success.

Thank you to you, the reader of this book. I wrote this book to empower you. I am excited and grateful that I can help you start your journey to success, to create online and grow rich.

Foreword

Do you dream of the day when you will earn a living from your creativity and quit your day job? What would your dream life be like if you had location freedom, time freedom and best of all, financial freedom? In *Create Online and Grow Rich: How You Can Escape the 9 to 5, Have Time Freedom, and Do What You Love*, Elke takes you on a journey of self-discovery, empowerment and transformation, while providing you with the system and proven plan you need to follow in order to make your dream a reality.

You will learn to develop a new mindset about how you can profit from your creativity and how to use this to your advantage. Elke will help you overcome your fears, limiting beliefs, and money blocks, while focusing on how you can monetize your creative abilities in the online space. Whether you are a graphic designer, artist, photographer or digital creative, in this book, Elke will inspire you, motivate you, and guide you through the steps you need to take to begin your journey to create online and grow rich.

Elke is the absolute best person to teach you how to create a wildly, profitable 6-figure online business using your creativity, because she has done it herself. She has made the mistakes for you, now you don't have to. Read her book and follow her advice so that you can unlock the riches your creativity can generate for you. Elke will ignite a passion in you to explore your previously untapped potential to generate wealth with your creativity that, once developed, will give you the opportunity to be financially free, doing what you love.

Raymond Aaron
New York Times Bestselling Author

Introduction – My Story

When I was growing up, I was told that the only way to be successful was to obtain a university degree. A degree would, in those days, guarantee a high-paying job and career that would set me up for life. So that is what I did.

After university, I landed what I thought was my ideal career job. My 9-to-5 job also had flexible work hours for working moms. I had a good salary and was promised a desirable career and salary advancement opportunities.

But my career dream job quickly became my career nightmare!

The nine-to-five hours were actually 9 until midnight, almost daily. I was required to travel out of town on week-long trips, once or twice a month. Plus, mandatory meetings started at 5 p.m., which was the time I was supposed to be getting my children from the babysitter.

The final straw was when I realized that no matter how well I did, I was only going to get a small yearly pay increase, and then it would be capped at an amount that was not worth the time sacrifice I was making being away from my family.

I needed to find a different way to earn money. I began mapping out what my dream job would look like. I definitely wanted time and location freedom. I wanted to work whenever I wanted and wherever I wanted, and still receive unlimited earnings for what I was doing.

I wanted to be there for my family all the time, not just to pick them up from the babysitter and to cook them dinner and put them to bed.

My job was in the science field, but I also love being creative. All my life, I had been told that I can't make money being creative. I had believed that lie and had given it my best shot, doing what my parents and society said would make me successful and happy. But I realized that I had to make myself happy by being creative, and that would lead to my own success.

Do you want to have these same freedoms that I wanted, and make money being creative doing what you love?

I wanted these freedoms so badly that I said, "There has to be a better way!"

So, I quit!

I made a commitment to myself that I was going to support my family using my creativity. I would sell my graphic design, photography, and artwork so that I could support my three young children and be there for them while they were growing up.

I was fortunate that I started selling lots of physical products right away. I thought I was doing well, until I did the math.

There were a lot of costs associated with creating the physical products, displaying them in brick and mortar galleries, paying gallery fees, exhibiting at art shows, and shipping the artwork to people all over the world. I realized that the amount of money that people were willing to pay for my art did not pay for all these extra costs.

I made zero profit, even though I had sold so many products.

That is when I had my *aha moment.*

I shouldn't be selling physical products; I should be selling digital products!

I started looking online to see if this was possible. This was in 2007, so there were just a few websites where you could sell your digital products online. I signed up to sell my art and photography on these sites.

But it was also when I discovered that there were other sites where I could post a digital image and sell it on different physical products. The companies on these websites would print, ship, bill, and handle customer service. All I had to do was post images and collect my royalties.

These sites included Fine Art America CafePress, Society6, Redbubble, and Zazzle.

I quickly realized that Zazzle was the best place to sell my digital art. I posted my photo of two polar bears on a button, which said, "Stop Global Warming."

I put it up for sale in my virtual store on Zazzle, and two days later, it had sold. I made my first sale on Zazzle!

I realized that if I could make $0.29 from the sale of a button, I could make more money.

I became obsessed with Zazzle.

I started putting up lots of products, and I thought I was doing really well; but in 2007, in my first year, I only earned $90. That wasn't even enough to get paid from Zazzle, because they had a $100 minimum payout.

So I kept working and testing things out.

Then, in 2008, I earned $2,380. Even though I had increased my earnings by 2000%, I couldn't seem to reach 5 figures in earnings, no matter how hard I tried.

But I was determined to succeed. I definitely did not want to go back to a cubicle, working for a boss and sitting in traffic for 2 hours every day to get back and forth from work.

Instead, I focused on my vision board. It had a picture of my family, which was my main motivation, a picture of the beach that I wanted to be on when I travelled with my family, and a picture of a computer that was spewing out money from the screen, just to give me a visual impression of how I wanted to make my money online.

I also spent a great deal of time testing and trying different things out to improve my product inventory, online marketing, and business strategy to see if these changes would make me more money on Zazzle.

After finally figuring out how Zazzle works, I had my first 5-figure earnings year, in 2009.

Spoiler alert! Even though Zazzle is not a get-rich-quick scheme, if you started on Zazzle today, it would not take you as long as it took me. You still have to do the work, but times are different, and now you can use a step-by-step proven program.

Back to my story....

My Zazzle earnings grew every year after that, and soon reached 6-figures.

Keep in mind, these numbers are my Zazzle earnings or payouts. Since I set my royalty at 10%, this means my business was generating over a million dollars in yearly Zazzle sales.

What other online business model can generate over 1 million dollars in sales, every year, for more than 7 years in a row, with no physical inventory, and no costs except your internet and computer, where you are working about 4 hours a month?

At the time of writing this book, I have sold over 10 million dollars' worth of Zazzle products, and have personally earned over 1 million dollars from my Zazzle business.

I figured out how to sell well on Zazzle.

I was featured on Zazzle's special 10th anniversary page as the top seller on Zazzle, selling over $25,000 dollars' worth of Zazzle products in one week. You can check it out at this link: https://www.zazzle.com/10th.

What was different from when I first started and these later years of success? I realized that it takes more than opening up a Zazzle store and randomly adding thousands of products.

The secret to achieving 6-figure and 7-figure sales on Zazzle is to use a proven plan and have a mentor.

Through my own struggles and failures, I learned and improved what to do until I had created my own proven plan that I could follow with confidence and ease. The 5 Step Profit Plan™ is my proven plan. It has consistently worked for me over the years, despite many changes on Zazzle that have negatively impacted other Zazzle designers who were not using my proven plan.

So, here is the good news for you. I have done the years of work for you. I have struggled and failed in order for you to learn the lessons and figure out what needs to be done to achieve success on Zazzle.

Now, year after year, I am consistently reaping the benefits of faithfully using The 5 Step Profit Plan™. I am living my dream life because I create online and grew rich. I have paid off my house. I have put my kids through school. I am debt-free. I take month-long vacations to amazing places in the world— all because my Zazzle business generates a consistent passive income for me.

Now it is your turn to create online and grow rich.

In this book, I take you on your own journey of self-discovery, empowerment, and transformation, while providing the perfect creative online business choice and the simple, proven 5 steps that you can take to begin your journey to success.

Chapter 1:

What Does It Take to Create Online and Grow Rich?

"Success in life is 80% psychology and 20% mechanics—what you do doesn't matter if you aren't in the right mindset." - Tony Robbins

You might be surprised to find that in the very first chapter, I don't come right out and say what money-making tool or system it is that I used to become a millionaire. I will tell you that it's a long-term, passive income, online business model that you can take advantage of the same way I did.

But there are several important things I need to help you with first, to ensure that you are ultimately successful. Why? Because many people who have had the same opportunity as I have, for the same amount of time as I did, have not made a million dollars from it, like I have. That's when I realized that I was doing things differently—things that helped me become successful.

What is my secret to success?

Why did I earn over a million dollars in this business, while others did not?

Am I more creative? No!

Did I work harder than others? No!

Did I get special privileges that gave me an advantage over others? Absolutely not!

I am just an average person, who taught myself the techniques to be creative, and took advantage of this online opportunity.

The secret that makes me different than the others is that I created my own unique and proven 5 Step Profit Plan™, which I follow and use to generate the income I desire, year after year.

The good news for you is that now you can access this proven plan too. If you know you are ready to get started right away with step-by-step tutorials, and dive into building your online business, then go to this link https://elkeclarke.com/profit/ and enroll.

However, don't put this book down, or stop reading—even if you are already one of my students in the program, this book is a must-read.

Why this book is a must-read

Whether you have just discovered me, or already know who I am and are a student of mine, you will love this book and will find it extremely valuable.

I guide you through essential elements of The 5 Step Profit Plan™, and expand on the training I cover on my program. This is an interactive book, in which you will be taken on a journey of self-discovery as I reveal to you my secret to making money online as a creative. I teach you, inspire you, motivate you, and guide you so that you can also create online and grow rich, like I did.

You will love having this book as your go-to reference, one that you will read multiple times, with many earmarked corners where you came across amazing *aha moments.*

Plus, I have added blank pages at the end of each chapter for you to write notes and do the exercises that I ask you to do throughout the book. I look forward to taking this journey with you.

Let's get started!

The right mindset

It's all about being in the right mindset. Over the years, I learned a valuable lesson. I had to get my mind on board with my plan to become a millionaire.

Tony Robbins was absolutely correct when he said:

"Success in life is 80% psychology and 20% mechanics—what you do doesn't matter if you aren't in the right mindset."

It was only after I had the right mindset about money and my creativity, as well as being really clear about my "Why," that I began to see incredible success.

That is why, in this chapter, you are going to learn to:

1. Eliminate your money blocks
2. Believe that you can make money being creative
3. Determine your "Why"

These actions will help shape your mindset and allow you to maximize your ability to achieve your goal to create online and grow rich.

Throughout, there will be TAKE ACTION prompts. It is essential that you complete each of these to get you started on your journey to grow rich.

Eliminate your money blocks

I achieved my dream of becoming a millionaire by being creative and doing what I love. Now it is your turn. I am going to share with you my journey, the lessons I learned, and what I did to achieve my dream goal.

One of the biggest lessons I had to learn came as a complete surprise to me. I did not realize I had money blocks. I didn't even know what money blocks were. I just assumed everyone thought like I did about money, and how you can get more of it. I certainly did not know that I was causing my own failure because I had a bad relationship with money! How can someone have a relationship with money?

But I kept failing in my business until I realized that my attitude towards money was so negative that I could not receive it.

With a background in science, I thought this *feeling* or *relationship* concept about money was extremely out there in La-La Land. I found it hard to believe at first. But as I did more digging, I came to realize that there was so much scientific proof about the law of attraction being at play, with not only attracting money, but anything else in life.

In order for you to achieve your millionaire status goal, you need to have the right mindset about money. You need to become comfortable talking about it, as well as feeling good about it. This is even harder for us creative types who have limiting beliefs about how we can generate income and how much we are supposed to earn.

Every person, including you, has a complex relationship with money. Your beliefs about money have been imprinted into your subconscious from early childhood, by your parents and circumstances in your life. These limiting beliefs are one of the key reasons why we are not all millionaires.

It's time for you to break the cycle

The first step you need to take to make money is to change your relationship with money: how you feel about making money, what you believe about people who have money, and what you think you need to do to make money.

Do these statements or sayings *feel* true to you as a gut reaction?

- *The love of money is the root of all evil.*
- *Money doesn't grow on trees.*
- *Rich people are greedy and corrupt.*
- *You have to work hard for money.*
- *Starving artist*

If you said yes to any of these, then these are your beliefs about money, at your subconscious level. I am sure you can think of others.

TAKE ACTION
I want you to take a moment right now and write down your limiting beliefs about money, in the "Notes" section, at the end of this chapter.

You might think these statements are true facts about money. But they are only *your* truths. Other people have different truths about money. You might ask yourself: "How can there be different truths about money?" What you think are truths are only your own unique beliefs about money, based on your experience and upbringing.

Luckily, since these statements are not absolute truths, you have the power to change your beliefs about money.

To become a successful creative millionaire, you must alter your relationship with money by changing your money beliefs.

3 steps to break through your money blocks

STEP 1
Be aware and open to questions: "What is not working for you? What belief or thought about money created this situation of lack?"

STEP 2
Accept the fact that what you have right now is in existence and your reality because of your current beliefs about money. It is hard to swallow because I certainly did not consciously want or ask for my own bad financial situation. But consider this: The beliefs you have now are obviously not working for you; otherwise, you would already have what you want.

STEP 3
Look for examples of abundance in the lives of other people (or your own), in order to begin changing your beliefs about what is possible in your relationship with money. These experiences can you help imprint new beliefs about money in your subconscious mind, which you will then have as your new money truths.

Think of abundance

There is an unlimited amount of abundance in this world, for which you can be grateful.

You can switch your previous money beliefs to ones that will allow abundance to come to you. The negative statements I mentioned earlier can be turned around to positive statements:

- *Money can be used for good.*
- *There is an abundance of money.*
- *Rich people are good and give back.*
- *Money does not equate to effort.*
- *Thriving artist*

TAKE ACTION
Write in the "Notes" section at the end of this chapter, what you want your new beliefs to be about money.

If you were raised in an environment of lack, then that is how you see the world now. You have to look for examples of abundance, and this will make you feel grateful for all that you have in life.

The big secret is that once you are filled with gratitude, you are in the vibration or emotion of receiving, which will allow you to receive more abundance, in all aspects of your life, not just money.

TAKE ACTION
Read my "Case Study" at the end of this chapter to get more details about how changing my relationship with money, busting my money blocks, and looking for abundance increased the flow of money into my life.

In the "Notes" at the end of this chapter, write down your own money limiting beliefs story. Then use the **3 Steps to Break Through Your Money Blocks (above)** *to help you work through at least one of your major money blocks or limiting beliefs.*

The sooner you tackle this major component, the sooner you will be on your way to making your millionaire dream a reality.

Believe that you can make money being creative

cre·a·tive
krē'ādiv
adjective
1.
relating to or involving the imagination or original ideas, especially in the production of an artistic work.
"Change unleashes people's creative energy."

noun
informal
1.
a person who is creative, typically in a professional context.

Are you creative? Of course, you are. Everyone is creative on one level or another. You have imagination, original ideas, and you can create original works, and you love being creative. So, yes! You are creative.

The problem is that society has instilled beliefs on you as a creative, which you also have to overcome. These are beliefs regarding who can determine if your work has value, and what type of financial payment you are supposed to receive for your work and time.

In fact, the worst is the *starving artist* phrase, which labels people, and assumes people who want to earn a living being creative cannot succeed. If you look for examples of artists, who have become wealthy from doing what they love, you will find many examples in our present society.

It is time for you to believe that you can earn as much money as you want being creative.

The cool thing about being creative in today's world is that you don't even have to go the traditional route artists like photographers, sculptors, painters, or graphic designers take. Sure, that is still an option for you, but with today's technology, the rules have totally changed.

You can be a self-taught creative, thanks to the Internet. You can build your reputation the traditional way in your field, or you can have a following you build up because you have a blog, website, or YouTube channel or Facebook page. You don't even have to create the traditional works of art or photography to be successful. There are so many other ways that people will pay you for your creativity.

It is a fabulous time to be a creative. Best of all, you can make money being creative in so many non-traditional ways online.

This new age of opportunity is why I was able to create online and grow rich.

I graduated university with a degree in sciences. The only traditional art training that I ever had was an art class I took as an elective in high school.

I am self-taught and use the Internet to make money using my creativity. Now you can too.

One of the biggest hurdles for me was overcoming my limiting beliefs about what I could achieve as a creative.

MY PAST CREATIVE LIMITING BELIEFS:

- My creativity is not good enough.
- I can't compete with others who have had formal training.
- My work is not worth very much.
- I have to sell my art and photography in traditional ways to make money.

TAKE ACTION
What are your limiting beliefs? Take a few minutes to write 3 or 4 of these beliefs in the "Notes" section at the end of this chapter.

As with my money blocks, I had some serious limiting beliefs about how successful I could be using my creativity. From a young age, whenever I was doing something creative like drawing, painting, or photography, my parents would tell me that I wouldn't make money with my creativity, and that I should focus on science or business.

By the time I was an adult, I was convinced that their belief was the truth. This belief was also reinforced by so many cues in society.

To be successful...

- Be a doctor!
- Be a lawyer!
- Go into business! You'll be set for life.
- Don't be a creative!
- You can't make money from art or photography! Those are hobbies.
- Get a real job.

Have you experienced a similar scenario? Have you been told any of these statements when you discuss your dream of being a success by being creative?

It seems odd that most people have these strong beliefs about what a creative can accomplish, especially when there are so many present-day artists who are millionaires or even billionaires, like Damien Hirst. These successful creatives did not let these limiting beliefs hold them back. Instead, they looked for innovative ways to crush these limiting beliefs.

Obviously, you and I are not Damien Hirst, but that does not mean we can't be rich using our creativity. In fact, I am proof that the average person, with average creative ability, can use opportunities available today to earn over a million dollars.

That means you have this opportunity too.

I will reveal my secret soon, on how you can earn money from your creativity. But first, I want to stress that my success is not just the means or mechanics of what I used to make money. A huge component was my mindset.

I credit my success to changing my limiting beliefs to my current liberating beliefs about making money using my creativity.

MY CURRENT CREATIVE LIBERATING BELIEFS:
- My creativity is abundant and valuable.
- I can teach myself and be good at anything creative.
- I receive the money I desire for my creativity.
- I always find new and unique ways to receive money for my creativity.

TAKE ACTION
Use my examples listed above, of my creative liberating beliefs, to come up with your own NEW CREATIVE LIBERATING BELIEFS. Write them in the "Notes" section at the end of this chapter.

Surround yourself with positive influencers

Once I had the courage to believe in myself and stopped believing what other people around me were saying, I started seeing the success I wanted for myself.

What about you? Do you have negative influencers who are constantly telling you about their own creative limiting beliefs?

Do the people around you tell you daily that you can't make money with your creativity? Or do they tell you stories of creative people that they know who failed. Or have they themselves tried and failed to make money being creative?

Do you want these negative influencers imprinting these beliefs into your subconscious? Of course not! Maybe you didn't even notice that this was happening to you. Luckily, you can easily change this.

Your job is to imprint onto your brain your new creative liberating beliefs.

Search out examples of people who are successful in art, photography, and graphic design. Find people who are not your typical role model. I want you to be realistic. You are most likely not the next Damien Hirst, but you are the next average, creative person who just also happens to believe that you can be a millionaire doing what you love.

Maybe that is why you bought this book: because you subconsciously already knew you needed proof that your dream is possible. After all, I am proof that you can become a millionaire being creative. Plus, I am right here, cheering you on. I know you can do it.

TAKE ACTION
There are 3 actions you need to take for this section.

- Look for positive role models that you can use to help convince you that your new creative liberating beliefs are true. Find people who have achieved your dream goal. Watch videos, read books, or look in the news to find examples of people who are successful being creative in unique ways.
- Surround yourself with people who have a positive outlook and will believe in your ability to reach your goal.
- Find a mentor who has accomplished what you want to do and can help guide you on your journey to success. Contact them, and start being mentored by them today.

Your road to millionaire status starts with defining your "WHY"

"There are only two ways to influence human behavior: you can manipulate it or you can inspire it. Very few people or companies can clearly articulate WHY they do WHAT they do."
– Simon Sinek

There are many examples to support that the reason great leaders became successful is because they had clearly defined their reason, or their "WHY". They were striving to achieve a particular goal. Simon Sinek demonstrates that clearly in his book, *Start with the Why: How Great Leaders Inspire Everyone to Take Action.*

It's time to define your "WHY".

Even though I am not a leader of a big corporation, I still took this advice seriously because I wanted to succeed in my own business. Let's be honest. If you don't know why you are putting your time and effort into challenging yourself to reach your million-dollar goal, then you will have a hard time staying motivated to keep going when you need to face the challenges or overcome the obstacles in your way.

Knowing your "WHY" will help you:

- Be inspired to excel and maintain a positive mindset
- Make decisions about your business with more clarity and certainty
- Deal with the setbacks in a more positive and productive way
- To keep striving to reach your ultimate goal over a longer period of time

My secret to success was to clearly define WHY I was striving to reach my million-dollar earnings goal. My "WHY" was to stay home with my kids while still earning a substantial passive online income. Being there for my kids, and having the time, freedom, and financial freedom to fully experience that time in my life and their lives, was my "WHY".

Now that my children are grown, my "WHY" has changed to having no debt and the freedom to only work if I want to, when I want to, and where I want to. I am pleased to say that defining my "WHY" allowed me to focus on what is important, and gave me the strength to push onwards with a positive mindset to reach my goal.

I now have zero debt. My house is paid off. I paid for my kids' education. I have the time freedom to be with friends and family when I want. I travel all over the world, for months at a time. Best of all, I still earn a 6-figure, passive income from my creativity with my online business.

Now it is your turn. What is your WHY?

TAKE ACTION
In the "Notes" section at the end of this chapter, write down your "WHY". What is your reason behind wanting to make money or to build your business? It could be similar to some of the reasons I mentioned, but it can also be something totally different.

You might want to prove that you can make the money you want by being creative. It might be to provide an income for early retirement. It might be to travel the world (young or old) while still earning money. You might want to volunteer, and need to find a way to support yourself.

There are so many reasons that could be your "WHY". They are all correct because your "WHY" is uniquely your own.

But make sure to choose only the one that you feel in your gut is the deepest, most passionate "WHY" of all of the items you might have listed.

Case Study

My story about money blocks, finding my WHY, and valuing my creativity

The money blocks I inherited

When I was young, I loved to draw and take photographs. I was creative in many ways and found hours of enjoyment being creative. We were a typical middle class family. My parents had to work hard for everything that they ever achieved. Like any typical parent, they wanted more for me than they could achieve in their lives. They were convinced that the only way I would ever be successful is if I became a doctor or lawyer. Making money from being creative was something that they discouraged at every opportunity they could get.

My parents' beliefs about how to make money were also typical money block beliefs, which I, not knowing any better, believed to be the truths about money.

Money truths like...Hard work is the only way to make more money. Rich people are corrupt. There is a finite number of ways to make money. There is only so much money to go around. ....You get the picture. So, for me, as a teenager, I had begun to believe these truths my parents taught me about money.

I want you to understand that I love my parents, and I don't blame them for imprinting these money blocks on me. They were taught these beliefs about money by their parents, and their parents before them. You should also not blame your parents or circumstances growing up.

The way to move forward is to break free and create your own new beliefs for yourself, like I did.

Breaking down your money blocks, and imprinting new money beliefs, takes time. Be patient. It not only takes a while to fully understand what your money blocks are, but then you have to make it a new belief habit. Habits typically take 21 to 30 days of daily repetition to start to set in. Even then, new habits have to be constantly re-enforced. But knowing the issue is half the battle, because now you can stop yourself when you go down that path of your old money beliefs that you think are true but really are not. They are only your beliefs, which can be changed.

It took quite some time for me to break my money blocks, because the way I make money now, from my creativity, was not even around until a little over 10 years ago. So I continued on the traditional route of going to university and getting a graduate degree. I got a job in the pharmaceutical industry, and I thought all was going to be fine: I had listened to my parents; I had a good job; I was making good money—but I was miserable.

I needed to define my "WHY"

I was good at what I was doing, and really proud of all of my accomplishments in my job. But I was living my parents' "WHY", not my own "WHY". So when the going got tough, I did not have the mindset and drive to be passionate and committed to achieving my goal of my career in the pharmaceutical industry.

I was working long hours, travelled at least 2 weeks a month, always seemed to have meetings right when I should be picking up my kids from the babysitter, spent many hours stuck in traffic, plus there was a limit to how much I could earn. I was frustrated and stressed, and felt like the job, even though it was rewarding, was not allowing me to live my life. My life was dictated by my work, and I was not happy. Something had to change.

That is why I quit my job and finally committed to pursue my passion of making money from my creativity. I wanted to be home with my young family. I was finally listening to my "WHY".

With my "WHY" clearly defined, I set out to find ways to support my family with my creativity. It was a struggle, but I was passionate and driven to succeed, because I always had my "WHY" to keep me moving forward, despite any setbacks.

I had to clearly define the value of my creativity

I learned a valuable lesson on my journey to success, monetizing my creativity.

Be open to different and new possibilities, and value your creativity.

If it wasn't for this lesson, I don't think I would have ever even taken the journey and path that I did to become an online millionaire.

At first, I tried traditional ways to make money from my paintings and photography. I participated in art shows. I had art hanging in galleries. I sold my physical paintings through my website and other art websites online. The problem was that I did not price my art high enough because I did not feel my creativity had value. It was only once I wasn't so desperate to sell my art at any cost to be validated, that sales were brisk.

There is more to this story, because I did not become a millionaire selling my physical art and photography. But you will have to read on in the next chapter to find out how my story unfolds, and how you too can make money with your creativity.

But before you read the next chapter, I want you to understand how much influence your mindset has over your overall success. Remember, Tony Robbins teaches that success is 80% psychology and 20% mechanics. I use his quote, but through my own journey, I experienced exactly the same thing. It took me a long time to realize that. I just kept doing the mechanics of working harder and longer, but never accomplishing my goal.

After achieving success and reflecting on my journey, I realized that it was only after I had dealt with my money blocks, valued my creativity, and was clear on my "WHY", that I, as a solo entrepreneur, could achieve millionaire status using my creativity.

I encourage you to save yourself a lot of time and grief. Learn from my story. Feel confident that you too can eliminate your money blocks, be confident in the value of your creativity, and stay true to your "WHY". These helped me tremendously on my journey to success and can help make the difference for you as well.

Elke's Secret to Success

Let your "why" dictate your choice of business.

Summary

In this chapter, I covered how to eliminate your money blocks, be confident in the value of your creativity, and stay true to your "WHY". These 3 main points are vital components in the overall success of your online business.

I am so excited that you have come this far: altering your mindset about money, and your belief in your creative value, and determining your why.

You are now ready to move on to explore how you will make money from your creativity, and discover my secret to success. In the next chapter, I will provide you with your options on how to make money with your creativity.

Notes:

Chapter 2:

Assess Your Options to Make Money Being Creative

"Business art is the step that comes after art. I started as a commercial artist, and I want to finish as a business artist. Being good in business is the most fascinating kind of art. During the hippie era, people put down the idea of business. They'd say; "money is bad" and "working is bad." But making money is art, and working is art—and good business is the best art." – Andy Warhol

Good business is the best art

In the quote above, by Andy Warhol, he eloquently expresses these exact mindset issues that most people have about art, and which hold them back. The right mindset about making money from your art is the key to your success.

I have already covered some of these mindsets in Chapter 1. Now, in Chapter 2, you will learn about the business side of art, and the mindset you need about business art, so that you can make the decisions and take the actions you need in order to be successful at monetizing your creativity.

I am going to show you that there are much better options than the traditional way of selling art, in which a physical product is sold in a physical environment. I will go one step further to convince you that selling physical products in a virtual environment (i.e. online) is better, but it is still not the perfect business model to achieve a substantial passive income.

Before I tell you what business model worked for me, you also need to shift your mindset about how your creativity can provide you income. All of this is up next in this chapter, so let's get started.

Debunking the *physical product, physical selling* business model

You might have had some sort of level of success selling your physical creative products in brick and mortar type venues. This strategy is what I am going to call the ***physical product, physical selling*** business model.

If you are a painter, photographer, or graphic designer, who is currently trying to sell your original artworks on physical products, you are probably well aware of the limitations to this business model—even though it seems to be the method of choice when an artist first decides to make money with their creativity.

You may have tried to sell your physical works in or at:
- Your own brick and mortar gallery or store
- Commercial brick and mortar art galleries

- Studio tours
- Outdoor and indoor art shows
- Restaurants and cafes
- Public spaces like community centers, libraries, and town halls
- Any other creative ways to get your works to be seen

Let's face it, there are many negatives to using these physical venues to sell your physical art.

These negatives include:
- Your upfront cost and investments
- Factors limiting the potential growth of your business

Your upfront costs and investments

The money you have to lay out, or *invest,* in your business before you even make a cent, is a huge negative to this business model of *physically selling your physical goods.*

Yes, I agree it is the traditional way that artists have as a way to sell their products, but I want you to consider who is receiving the money.

Let's look at your upfront costs:

- **Supplies:** Materials to create the physical products for sale
- **Inventory Creation and Storage:** Creating and maintaining an inventory of originals, prints, and other merchandise

- **Fees:** Fees to display your physical product, whether that is in the form of rent for your store, gallery commissions, or entrance fees to art shows
- **Time:** Your valuable time is used to man your gallery or store, or art show booth, and move your physical products to and from venues. This time is costing you lost revenue because you could be using it to create more inventory.

So far, the only people making money from your *physical product, physical selling* business model are: the landlord of your store; the gallery owners, art show event organizers, and the companies making your reproductions and other merchandise.

You have not made any money because you have not sold anything.

Factors limiting the potential growth of your business

In this *physical product, physical selling* business model, you are making a huge investment for very little return, because all of these physical venue options have many limiting factors, including:

- **Limited exposure:** The number of people you can reach as potential customers is extremely low and is restricted to geography.
- **Restricted prices:** The prices you can charge are dictated by your location and selling situation.
- **Limited product numbers showcased:** The number

of physical pieces that you can showcase is limited due to physical space.

- **Not the correct target customer:** The style of your work may not even be the type of work the customers in or at these venues are looking for. So you think you are receiving viewers of potential buyers, but really you are not.

Ultimately, it is a numbers game with buyers' habits mixed in. You need a certain number of people who are actual buyers to see your work, because only a fraction on them will buy. It is usually a low percentage, like 2 to 5%. That means this business model does not allow you to scale up to reach the dollar number you need to earn a substantial income.

You have put your creativity and money into this business, but the profits for your time and investment, using this business model, may be less than you realize.

TAKE ACTION:
Can you relate or have had experience selling your art, whatever that may be, using this *physical product, physical selling* business model?

In the "Notes" section, I want you to write down what your Total Earnings, Total Expenses, and resulting Profit were from your "physical product, physical selling" business model experience.

Profit = Total Earnings - Total Expenses

Then I want you to estimate the number of hours you spent, so that you can come up with your hourly wage.

Your Hourly Wage = Profit in Dollars / Time in Hours

You might be shocked to find out how little this business model was paying you. What I want you to realize is that the time, effort, and costs you put into this way of making money from your creativity is limited and not scalable. There are only so many hours in a day, and your physical ability to create and churn out product is also limited.

Case Study – My Story

In my journey as an artist and creative, I realized early on that the *physical product, physical selling* business model was not going to work for an average artist like myself, who wanted to make a consistent 6-figure income, year after year. After all, that meant I had to make a PROFIT of at least $100,000!

I was selling paintings, framed photographs, and other textile goods. I was working extremely hard. I was selling and making money, but I realized my hourly wage was so low that I was making less than minimum wage. Plus, my profits were non-existent.

It was not worth continuing with this business model.

What about you?

Are you like me and want a better business model to make substantial income using your creativity?

I have convinced you to change your mindset about selling physical products in physical venues.

Let's move on to the next business model: *physical product, virtual selling.*

Is the *physical product, virtual selling* online business model profitable?

Let's look at the *physical product, virtual selling* business model. In this business model, an online platform of some sort is used to showcase your physical products for sale. These platforms can be your own website, online galleries, online marketplaces, and social media sites. The key here is that all that has changed from the previous business model is the venue you are selling in, or in this case, selling on.

Online venues, which you can use to sell your physical works, have been broken down into 5 main categories below:

- Your own website, with ecommerce capability, like Shopify or WordPress
- Art marketplaces and online art galleries - like Saatchi
- Art, Artplode, Artfinder, and Yessy
- Large seller marketplaces, like Etsy, Amazon, and eBay

- Digital art marketplaces, like Big Stock Photo or Envato
- Social media sites, such as Facebook, Pinterest, and Instagram

Each of these 5 categories of online venues have both benefits and disadvantages, to help you achieve your goal to successfully monetize your creativity.

Benefits
- Wider reach worldwide because now your items are searchable on the Internet
- Increased number of potential customers because you have access to existing clients on a particular online platform, even if they are not your customers
- The potential to showcase an unlimited number of products (unless there is a fee per item) provides a higher chance of sales.
- Reduced time and effort. You have more time to create or promote because you don't have to physically be somewhere to sell your art.

Disadvantages
- There are still costs, including fees to use sites, and/or commissions on sales.
- You must still deal with inventory creation and storage, shipping the physical product, and customer service.
- You must promote your products and build your brand in order to be found online.

- There is more competition. A customer can choose from a larger selection during one buying experience because there are many more artists in some of these platform categories (except for your own website), compared to a physical gallery or art show.
- Shipping cost is a big factor in whether a sale is finalized. The buyer may not want to pay the high costs of international shipping, resulting in loss of the sale.
- Other than your own website, any of these platforms can shut down or change the rules at any time, which can shut your business down overnight or force you to adhere to their new policies, which can affect your market reach and expenses.
- Some sites are easy to use, but others require a time investment to get up and running with the tech side of things.

Even though I have used online venues in each of these 5 categories to sell my physical products, this is not what made me a millionaire.

You may have also tried to sell your physical products on these venues, and wondered why you were not making the money you thought you would.

The potential reasons for this lack of consistent substantial sales can be explained by a number of limiting factors. These can work together to cap your ability to generate the volume of sales required to reach your target earnings goal.

Limiting factors of the *physical product, virtual selling* business model

- Cost of continual physical inventory creation
- Storage costs of unsold inventory
- Only one possible sale per physical item
- Delay in manufacturing due to artist's time creating additional products (There is only one of you, and only so many hours in the day.)

Although there are always exceptions to this business model, for the average artist like myself, I realized I would never be a millionaire with this approach.

I still needed to keep investing in more product creation and inventory storage until an item sells. Even if my online presence created a rush of sales, I would not be able to fill all the orders quickly because I would need time to create each new piece, leading to customer dissatisfaction and decreased sales.

The most important limiting factor of this business model of selling original physical art is that you can only make money once, from something you spent a very long time making. Unless your product sells for an extremely high price, which is unlikely for the average artist, you are again making less than minimum wage, for zero profit.

It all comes down to the numbers, again. Even though you may not like looking at your numbers, it is the key to you switching from financing your creative hobby to turning your creativity into a thriving business.

TAKE ACTION:
Have you used any online platforms to sell your physical products?

In the "Notes" section, I want you to write down what your Total Earnings, Total Expenses, and resulting Profit were from your "physical product, virtual selling" business model experience.

Profit = Total Earnings - Total Expenses

Then I want you to estimate the number of hours you spent, so that you can come up with your hourly wage.

Your Hourly Wage = Profit in Dollars/Time in Hours

Your aha moment

By now, you might have realized that even though you have increased your market reach and have more time for product creation, you are most likely still not turning a profit.

Ultimately, the reality is that unless your product is priced in the thousands, you will not make a profit selling a physical product that took you a long time to make.

Also, selling the original product only allows you to make money off of your effort one time. That means you have to continually make more original artwork that sells frequently. That is hard to do unless you have a famous reputation, and people will buy your products only because of your name.

Case Study – My Story

I had to face reality. I was still not profitable, let alone earning 6-figures, even though I was doing it all:

- I was using multiple online opportunities to sell my art.
- I had my own art website.
- I was using social media to promote my site and sell.
- I was represented by a number of online art galleries, including the Saatchi Gallery, one of the world's largest online art galleries.
- I also had my physical art for sale on 4 other major online art galleries, of which only 1 is still in existence today, 10 years later.

I was taking advantage of all the online options to sell my physical original art.

At that time, I was well represented all over the Internet and in different markets. If I did a Google search, my art came up and dominated the top search results. My art sold well, and I was ecstatic to be recognized and have art in private collections worldwide.

But the numbers do not lie. When I did the math, I was not profitable, even after trying to make this *physical product, virtual selling* business model work for over 2 years.

It was time to regroup and make the decision that this business model did not work for me.

I had to find another way: a way to make money without so much upfront cost and time investment in the production, and a way to sell my one product over and over again.

I needed an evergreen-sales, low cost inventory, high profit solution, in order to profit from my creativity.

Selling digital creative products online is profitable and sustainable

That is when I discovered print on demand (POD) online platforms. Back in 2007, this concept and a handful of companies were just emerging to provide this service online.

The way it worked was that I uploaded my artwork, photography, and graphic art onto virtual products in a virtual store, with my own URL subdomain on each platform, so customers could see the products online.

Once the customer paid for the item, the company would print my digital image onto the item the customer bought. That is where the print on demand term comes from. The physical printed product would only be printed once the customer paid for it (or demanded it).

In 2007, the only other way to sell copies of any original artwork and photography on flat surfaces was using giclée prints. It was the way big name artists were making a fortune selling limited editions. Since I was not at that level, I had to find an alternative to investing even more money in making giclée-type prints of my original artwork.

When I found sites online that would make the prints for me only once a customer bought them, I realized that this changed everything.

I did not have to pay more money to make prints that may or may not be purchased, and the customer had already paid for the print before it was made. Plus, the online company shipped the product for me, billed the customer, handled customer service, and paid me my royalty, which I had control to set.

PODs really changed my mindset of how I could profit from my creativity.

The *Virtual Product, Virtual Selling, Evergreen Passive Income* business model is profitable

When you look up *Print on Demand*, or POD, you will find that companies with that label or distinction are not all the same. But the ones I found, back when I started moving my business into the *Virtual Product, Virtual Selling, Evergreen Passive Income* business model, are listed below:

- Zazzle
- Fine Art America
- Redbubble

These companies were and still are focused on promoting artists in their own unique ways, using their online platforms. On each site, you can also sell more than just art related products, like canvases and posters. These sites provide a wide range of products on which you can add your digital image, and offer it for sale.

In essence, you are licensing your work to these "Print on Demand" companies and receiving royalty payments each time your image is printed and sold on a product.

My aha moment

This was a total mindset shift for me because, by using the *Virtual Product, Virtual Selling, Evergreen Passive Income* business model, I could actually make a profit.

I just had to make my creative product once, whether that was a painting, photograph, or digital design. Then I would use the easy to use tools on these POD ecommerce platforms to add the digital image of my design to the virtual products in my virtual online stores.

In essence, I was staging my image for the customer to see what it would look like on a canvas, poster, or any other item I wanted to sell my image on. I could do this for free, and set my royalty rates, and the items would be available to be purchased by millions of people all over the world.

The best part was that this could happen over and over again.

I had found an evergreen passive way to earn money with my creativity.

I had gone from making zero profit to making huge profits, because:

- I cut out the time and money to physically sell my products = **more productivity**
- I was able to provide customers with as many copies as they wanted, without production delays = **more sales**
- I broadened my market reach by selling my design on many different products other than canvases and posters, which I could not have manufactured on my own = **increased product inventory and market share, without any capital investment**
- I put up the information in my virtual stores once, and then the products would sell over and over again without me doing any more work. = **the creation of evergreen passive income (it occurs over and over again without me doing any more than the initial work).**
- I had free time to make more original works or add more product offerings to my virtual stores = **my business is working for me instead of me working for my business**
- There are no limitations to my building my business to make as much money as I want = **scalable business model**

I had found my way of making a substantial profit while working less, with the "Virtual Product, Virtual Selling, Evergreen Passive Income" business model.

Let go of your artist ego. Create and sell what the customers want.

You have now come on my journey with me so far. I finally found a business model that works for me, as an average creative who wants to make a substantial passive income.

After all, my "WHY", for even starting this business in the first place was to be able to stay at home with my kids while passively earning a substantial amount of money to replace my day job salary.

I found a business model that worked for *me*, instead of me working for my business. So that was checked off.

But before I could move further, I had one more mindset shift to make.

I had to let go of my artist ego.

Yes, at that time, I was very much in the mindset of a typical artist. I thought my art should be purchased because people liked me as an artist and wanted to collect my work. I definitely had that type of clientele. The problem, though, was that I was not seeing the volume of sales I needed in order to make a substantial income with this set of customers.

I had to let go of my artist ego.

I was crushed when people bought my art only because it was the right color for their living room décor. Plus, I also felt my creativity was being smothered because, to make money, I had to make a painting in a color palette that I didn't want to.

I had to let go of my artist ego.

I was upset when people wanted a deep discount because they didn't want to pay the shipping costs. Somehow, they thought that, as an artist, I would be so desperate to sell my art at a deep discounted price.

I had to let go of my artist ego.

I was livid when I went to home décor stores and saw people buying cheap, poor quality, pixelated prints made in China, for double or triple the cost of my original artwork.

It became clear that artists, like myself, had to change their approach in order to make money with their creativity, selling to the general public.

To profit from this buying culture, I had to let go of my artist ego.

I will talk about this in greater detail in the upcoming chapters, but the essence of this mindset change was that I had to be less artsy and more businesslike in my approach.

If it was going to generate a sale for me, I would:
- Make my art in the trending colors
- Price my items based on market trends, but make sure I still made a profit by finding the right supplier

- Ensure I could supply items all over the world, without me paying for the shipping
- Provide the type of product type the buyer wanted my design on, without judgment that my art was beneath being on a particular product

Create and sell what the customers want.

Every single issue I experienced, trying to sell my art as art, I addressed and found solutions for them.

I was bringing my art to the buyers in ways that they were willing to buy it, with my artist ego taking backstage.

I am happy to say that this worked so well that my business quickly went from 5 figures to 6 figures in profit for me.

You do not have to be good at your craft to make money.

There is one more artistic mindset hurdle that you MUST overcome before I tell you the mechanics, or what I used to become a millionaire.

This might actually be the hardest for you to accept and change. So be easy on yourself, and just let me be your mentor.

Many of my students that are in my mentoring program (https://elkeclarke.com/profit/), find that this last mindset change is the most challenging for them to get their head around. It is, however, essential for you to conquer, for your success.

What is this artistic mindset hurdle?

You do NOT have to be:
- the best technically at creating your art
- the most popular artist, photographer, illustrator, graphic designer, etc.
- the most educated
- the most trained
- the most prolific
- the most recognized and acknowledged with awards and distinctions

You can be of average skill level and still be creative enough to design what the customer wants to buy.

It is so important that you value your artistic talents, no matter what level they are, and that you feel confident that your creativity will lead to you creating products that customers want to buy.

I love that this fact is true, because if it were not, I would still be struggling. Instead, I trusted that I had the artistic ability to create whatever I found the market was interested in, so that I could profit from my creativity.

That is what you also need to understand. I will talk more about this in the upcoming chapter, where I reveal what my secret to success is, and how you can use it too.

Elke's Secret to Success

The "Virtual Product, Virtual Selling, Evergreen Passive Income" business model is profitable for people who are willing to make money selling their creativity in unique ways.

Summary

In this chapter, I showed you, on my journey to millionaire status, how I have tried many different options to make a substantial income using my creativity. I have sold physical products in physical locations, as well as online. But the first time I made a profit was when I found the option to sell online without any investment cost to me. This business model was financially much more lucrative, but I also learned that I needed to change my artistic mindset to really become profitable.

In the next chapter, I will reveal which of these online platforms I used in order to make over a million dollars selling my creativity.

Notes:

Chapter 3:

The Undiscovered Secret to Create Online and Grow Rich

"Step out of the history that is holding you back. Step into the new story you are willing to create." – Oprah Winfrey

What is the undiscovered ecommerce secret that creatives, like you, can use to make money online?

In the last chapter, I showed you why the *Virtual Product, Virtual Selling, Evergreen Passive Income* business model is the best way to generate the most profit, while working the least amount of time, with the lowest amount of capital expense.

I will reveal to you which ecommerce platform works with this preferred business model, and is the one I still use to generate a 6-figure yearly income, using my creativity. The best part is that you can use this ecommerce platform as well, to build a long-term passive income.

In my 10 years of experience making money online, this ecommerce platform is the best one to use to set up your *Virtual Product, Virtual Selling, Evergreen Passive Income* business.

So, which ecommerce platform is the best undiscovered secret?

Where can you sell online and make money using your creative talents?

What ecommerce platform did I use to become a creative online millionaire?

The answer is Zazzle.

Zazzle is the undiscovered ecommerce secret to making money online with your creativity.

Zazzle is the ecommerce platform I used to become a creative online millionaire.

Not Shopify, not Amazon, not Etsy—nor any other print on demand (POD) option, like Fine Art America, CafePress, Redbubble, or Society6, to name a few—but Zazzle. If you have heard of some of these, or even tried them already, you will be amazed at the potential and benefits of Zazzle in comparison. Zazzle is the best option.

How can you make money online using Zazzle?

Besides being a great online marketplace where customers can design and manufacture their own unique products, Zazzle is an amazing ecommerce platform for creatives to make money online. Zazzle would not be what it is today without the ability to sell unique graphics, art, and photography on their products from creative designers. That is why Zazzle provides such a fantastic business opportunity for creatives, like me and you.

It's a win-win situation because Zazzle listens to the designers, and continually improves the platform and earning opportunities for designers.

There are actually 3 ways you can make money online with Zazzle, whether you are an artist, photographer, graphic designer, or just have a creative side.

You can make money on Zazzle by:

- Selling your creative designs on products that you list in your virtual Zazzle store. In essence you are licensing your designs to Zazzle for a royalty fee which you set, earning the royalty income when something sells.
- Promoting your Zazzle products and earning your set royalty income and 15% referral (affiliate) income when you drive external traffic to Zazzle and sell your own products.
- Promoting other Zazzle products and earning referral income of 15% (affiliate) when you sell anything offered for sale on Zazzle that is not your own designs.

Why is Zazzle the perfect online business model and opportunity?

The benefits to using Zazzle as your *Virtual Product, Virtual Selling, Evergreen Passive Income* business model are many. Zazzle takes care of all of the following parts of running a successful online business, which you would have to do by yourself if you were on your own or using a different ecommerce platform, like Shopify, Amazon, or Etsy. Plus, Zazzle has more advantages and opportunities for earning than Fine Art America, CafePress, Redbubble, or Society6.

Zazzle:

- Has a unique ecommerce platform with a patented one-of-a-kind design tool that customers can use to personalize and customize existing designs before purchasing.
- Has thousands of unique product types in multiple niches that you as the designer can use to add your designs to and sell in your virtual Zazzle store.
- Allows designers to add up to 100,000 products in their virtual store for free.
- Does not have an approval process, so you can sell your designs immediately.
- Keeps your product designs visible in the Zazzle marketplace for 18 months, even if the product has not been viewed, and will maintain public view of the product indefinitely if it has sold once.
- Allows you, the designer, to set your own royalty (from 5 to 99%).

- Creates partnerships with suppliers and manu-facturers to continually source new products.
- Ensures efficient and speedy production of purchased products.
- Arranges with shippers to deliver the finished product to the customer.
- Reaches millions of customers worldwide with its international website domains.
- Has an entire marketing team working to drive both paid and organic traffic to Zazzle worldwide domains.
- Takes care of customer billing and accounts receivable.
- Has a great customer service department and money back guarantee.
- Is a stable, privately held company, which started in 2005.
- Has continually improved its website and services for both the customer and the designers who sell on the site.
- Pays you your royalty and referral money monthly.

Zazzle is a great ecommerce opportunity because the platform has already taken care of so many aspects of selling online, compared to other ecommerce online shopping businesses you can use, like Shopify, Etsy, and Amazon.

Even though Zazzle has many benefits that make your life easier, you still need to work at it like any other business.

However, you can shorten the time it would normally take you to become successful on Zazzle, by using a proven plan of someone who has been successful on Zazzle already—someone who has tried and failed, but who has learned from their mistakes, and now has a proven plan that works for them.

TAKE ACTION:

Do you have experience selling your creativity using any of these online ecommerce platforms (Zazzle, Shopify, Amazon, Etsy, Fine Art America, CafePress, Redbubble, or Society6)? Are you making the amount of money you want from these websites?

In the "Notes" section in this chapter, I want you to create a table. On the far-left column of the table, list each of the above-mentioned online platforms that you have had experience with. Next to each online site, write the total amount of years you have spent on each one. Next to the years, write the total amount of money you have earned from each. Next to the total, put a check mark if you are happy with your result, or an "X" if you are not.

If you have never tried any of these online ecommerce platforms, after visiting each of the websites and researching them, next to each name on your table in the "Notes" section, put a check mark if you think you could make money on that platform, or an "X" if you don't feel that you could do it on your own and would need help to achieve success.

If you have used any of these platforms, you might find your review eye opening. Maybe you have made some money with one or some of these, but never with Zazzle. Or you may have made a small amount of money with some or all of the platforms but wish you could earn more for your efforts because you want to earn a living using ecommerce, instead of it being your side hustle.

Each platform presents different challenges that you need to overcome in order for you to achieve substantial success, and that is what stops people like you from becoming successful.

From my experience, Zazzle has the least challenges to overcome out of all of these, with the lowest financial risk.

Please understand that Zazzle, and these other platforms, are NOT get-rich-quick schemes. As with any successful business, it requires hard work and implementing the right plan of action for you to see results on each platform.

Compared to the other platforms listed above, the Zazzle ecommerce platform provides more opportunity for sales, and the monetary investment is lower, before you begin to see results.

That's why I recommend and use Zazzle. I will explain more of the benefits and how you can get started, in this chapter. But first, I want to share with you my Zazzle story, because if I can do it, you can too.

As a side note, if you are reading this and are saying, "Elke, I'm on Zazzle already and am not making money like you are. Why should I keep going with Zazzle?" My answer to you is, "It's not Zazzle. It's something that is stopping you from achieving success, which I can help you solve."

My Zazzle Story – From 29 Cents to Millionaire

Over the past 10 years, I have sold over 10 million dollars' worth of products (with my creative designs on them) through the Zazzle ecommerce platform. Because of my Zazzle sales, I have been paid out over 1 million dollars in royalties from Zazzle since starting in 2007.

I didn't tell you this to brag. I tell you this to inspire you and to let you know that I am not the only one who has achieved this level of income on Zazzle. But I am the only one who has made my earnings public. I am the only one who is mentoring and coaching people, like you, to make money on Zazzle.

Others who are making a substantial amount of money on Zazzle are afraid that they will earn less if there is more competition. That is why they keep Zazzle and their earnings a secret.

But that is a myth.

My 5 Step Profit Plan Program™ members are proof that you can start today, and with the right training and steps to follow, you can sell well on Zazzle.

Plus, by helping others, my personal Zazzle earnings have not been affected. There is an abundance of opportunity on Zazzle, so that you too can make money, starting today.

The reason this is possible for you is because Zazzle is always expanding their product lines, improving their platform, building more production facilities, and reaching more customers every day, worldwide. That means there is just as much opportunity today to earn money on Zazzle as there was 10 years ago when I started. In fact, there is even MORE opportunity for you than there was for me. Imagine your possibilities.

Let me tell you about my Zazzle journey highlights in numbers. Every year, since 2012, my creative designs generate over 1 million dollars in sales each year on Zazzle. Since I set my royalty at an average of 10%, this means that I have consistently earned a 6-figure passive income, yearly, on Zazzle.

I am featured on Zazzle as one of the top-sellers, selling over $25,000 worth of Zazzle products, with my designs on them, in one week. You can check it out at this link: https://www.zazzle.com/10th.

I reached Zazzle's top tier (Diamond) of their ProDesigner program, which recognizes the accomplishments of designers who sell on Zazzle.

It is great to be recognized for my accomplishments as a Zazzle Diamond ProDesigner, but it is the fact that I continue to generate a substantial passive income, year after year, using my creative designs on Zazzle, that matters to me the most.

But it wasn't always like this

Before Zazzle, I was working at an office job, using my education, and I was miserable. I was doing something I hated (even though I was good at it). I had to do a lot of travelling. I worked nights and weekends because there were cutbacks, and I was doing the work of 2 people. My work was supposed to have flex hours, but there were always mandatory meetings right at 5 p.m. when I was supposed to leave to pick up my kids from daycare. I was overworked and found out that I would be capped at a certain salary no matter what I accomplished in the future.

I asked myself, "Is this the best I can do to be happy and support my family?"

My priorities had also changed. I didn't want to miss out on any more important milestones in my children's lives. I started dreaming of staying home with my kids. I wanted to see them for more than an hour a day. They needed me, but I was not there for them. I was sending them to various babysitters and daycare to accommodate my job hours. The guilt was unbearable.

I began making a list of what I wanted in my dream job. I wanted to run an online business from home, using my creativity, and having location and time freedom to be with my kids. But I needed to make more money than I did in my day job. That seemed like an unachievable dream, especially since, back in 2007, online opportunities were just getting started and were not as common as they are today.

My dream came true for me because I persevered and did not give up.

TAKE ACTION:
What about you? What is your dream job?

In the "Notes" section of this chapter, write down the heading, "My Dream Job." Then spend some time really defining your dream job, and when you are ready, write it down under this header.

What did you realize? Is your ideal dream job to also work online and make money passively selling your creativity? Then this book is for you. Keep reading to find out how you can start your journey to achieve your dream job.

I found Zazzle and struggled a lot until I figured out how it works, but you don't have to.

When I first started trying to make money online, I signed up for and added products for sale to many different ecommerce platforms and Print on Demand (POD) online sites, including Zazzle.

I worked really hard, and had many products up online, but no sales. That was until I sold my first product on Zazzle. It was a button with a picture of 2 polar bears on it, which paid me 29 cents. Even though it was a small amount of money, I realized that this could work for me, and Zazzle was the platform to use. I just needed to figure out how to scale it up to make more money.

It was a difficult struggle at the beginning to figure out how Zazzle works and how I could make money using Zazzle effectively. But over the years, I worked on my strategy and perfected my plan that I followed. I started seeing more and more success.

Once I figured it out and had developed my proven plan, I religiously followed it because it was the key to my success. I called my plan The 5 Step Profit Plan™. When I implemented all 5 steps in The 5 Step Profit Plan™, into my Zazzle business, I saw huge increases in my sales and profits.

So now that my 5 Step Profit Plan VIP Mentoring Program™ members have my exact same 5 steps to follow, and me as their mentor to guide them, they are seeing results much faster than I did. They don't have to spend years figuring it out on their own.

The reason I struggled at the beginning was because I had no proven plan. I just added products for sale randomly to my Zazzle store, without any strategy, because I was desperate to make money. My earnings results reflected my lack of direction.

I only made $90 in earnings in my first year! I was extremely disappointed because I had worked so hard, but I realized working hard is not really the answer. I had to work effectively. In my second year, I had started to figure things out a bit more, and I earned $2,380.

But at this point, I was feeling a lot of pressure from my family. They told me I was wasting my time and that I should get a real job. That is when I made a commitment to finally figure Zazzle out. I needed to make it work for me so that I would make 6-figures a year consistently, to meet my income goal.

TAKE ACTION:
What about you? Are you feeling the pressure?

Do you have a Zazzle store(s) and are struggling like I was? Or are you trying some other online platform and not earning what you want?

In the "Notes" section of this chapter, write down the heading, "My Struggles." Then spend some time really thinking about why you are struggling, and then write these down under the header.

What did you realize your struggles are? Do you not have enough time? Is this your side hustle? Do you need a plan that works, to save you from wasting your precious little time that you have to devote to getting your business working for you? Are you not on the right platform? Are you already on Zazzle but need a proven plan of action that increases your earnings?

In the "Notes" section, below where you wrote your struggles, write in capital letters:

"I AM COMMITTED TO FIGURING OUT A WAY TO MAKE MONEY ONLINE WITH MY CREATIVITY."

Awesome! Now that you are committed, I want to let you know that I am committed to helping you. Remember, I have been where you are, and I have risen to the challenge. You can rise to the challenge as well. Plus, now you have a way to move forward faster, and with less headaches and heartaches.

I escaped the 9 to 5, have time freedom, and I do what I love, all because of my success on Zazzle.

In 2007, I knew that other designers were already making huge amounts on Zazzle, even though I was still struggling. I was looking for a mentor—someone I could get advice from who was doing well on Zazzle—who could help me move forward.

I was willing to pay someone, because I have paid other mentors in the past when I wanted to learn something new and become really good at it.

I did come across some people on the Zazzle forum who gave friendly but general advice. But there was no one who would tell me what products sold, what niches were popular, and what to do to earn a substantial income on Zazzle.

It was a lonely struggle, especially since there were no other entrepreneurs I could talk to who I knew and could trust their advice. There were no courses or programs on how to make money on Zazzle. I was on my own and tried everything to figure out how Zazzle worked so I could make money. I vowed that I would help people once I figured Zazzle out.

After trying many strategies, I finally started to see more successes than failures. I soon optimized my strategy that had begun to consistently work for me. I called it The 5 Step Profit Plan™. When I put the 5 steps into place in my Zazzle business, I went from making a few thousand dollars a year to earning 5-figures a year. Then, as my business grew, I started making 6-figures a year, consistently, despite the changes that constantly happen on Zazzle over the years.

In 2017, 10 years after I started, I became an online millionaire, solely by selling my graphic designs, art, and photography on Zazzle products. Since then, my income keeps growing every year. I owe my success to following The 5 Step Profit Plan™. If you would like to read more about my journey, please visit
https://elkeclarke.com/how-i-became-an-online-millionaire-with-zazzle/

My income from Zazzle has given me so many opportunities that I never dreamed I could have, but they have come true for me.

What my Zazzle income has allowed me to do:

- quit my 9 to 5 job
- stayed home with my kids while they were growing up
- was at every important event in my children's lives
- paid off my house
- put my kids through school (so my kids have no debt)
- be debt free
- travelled to many places in the world
- have the time freedom to experience and be there for my kids and family members

I am so grateful that I kept going and did not give up. My life is so much better now than it would have been without my income from Zazzle.

Plus, I get to be creative every day and make money.

TAKE ACTION:
What about you? Do you want any of these things that I have been able to do?

Whatever you instinctively answered, without thinking about it or filtering it, is your true "Why".

Go back to your "Notes" in Chapter 1, and find what you wrote under the heading, "Why". Is it still the same as what came to your mind as you were reading about the things I accomplished? Take a moment now to confirm your deepest desire, or your "Why". Revise your "Why" if necessary, and earmark it.

This "Why" is your reason that will keep you motivated and drive you to succeed, no matter what hardships or setbacks you encounter.

Come back to it often in these "Notes" to help motivate you and remind you of your reason for why you are working so hard and never giving up.

You have your "Why". Now you need your *success strategy*.

Do you think you would be successful if you:
- were committed to do the work needed?
- had a proven plan you could follow?
- had access to a mentor who is already successful at what you want to accomplish?
- had all 3?

In the "Notes" section of this chapter, write down the heading, "My Success Strategy." Then spend some time really thinking about what you have read so far. Then write down what you think you need to be successful selling your creativity.

Keep in mind the things you have learned in the last 3 chapters. You want to make money with your creativity online, using the best ecommerce platform. You also want to follow a proven plan to save time and see results sooner. Plus, you realize that you need a mentor, who has already done what you want to accomplish, for support, encouragement, and guidance, and to help you stay committed to working toward your goal.

Write the things out that you need for your success strategy, in your "Notes," so that they become imprinted in your mind. Next to each, write down what action step you need to take to put your strategy into action.

For example, if you wrote, "need an ecommerce platform...," you would add, "Check out Zazzle today. If I like it, create an account."

Or if you wrote, "Need a mentor...," you would add, "Check out Elke's mentoring program, and sign up if I like it and am committed to getting started."

Do that for each of your items on your "Success Strategy" list.

Why is Zazzle a unique and popular online shopping experience?

Zazzle is a one-of-a-kind, ecommerce platform, specifically a Print on Demand (POD) company, with unique features that make it the perfect choice for a creative, like you, to make money online.

I have already told you about these features, but now I want to tell you how shoppers experience Zazzle, and why they love shopping on the platform. After all, you can't make money if there are no shoppers on the platform you are using. But Zazzle makes it a great place to shop, so you can make money selling your designs.

If you were shopping as a customer, you would see Zazzle as an online marketplace, where you can buy unique designs posted for sale by indie designers, and brand names that you can further customize to make your own.

The customization is why Zazzle stands out from the rest of the PODs and ecommerce platforms like Amazon, Shopify, and Etsy. Zazzle allows customers to manufacture their own designs using the template designs they find on Zazzle.

Zazzle is the only POD site on which customers can customize and personalize their products before ordering. Plus, the customer can see exactly what it will look like before they buy.

Besides having this unique patented custom design and instant visualization tool, Zazzle also offers a wide range of products to print on, and they sell and ship internationally.

There are billions of different products and templates to choose from. Designers, including me, have added designs virtually onto products and posted them for sale in the Zazzle marketplace. Products range from stationery for occasions and business, to home décor, including art, to clothing and accessories, to sports accessories, to holiday accessories, to edibles, and much more.

Once the order is placed and paid for, Zazzle uses the digital file to print the actual product ordered, and ships the item to the customer. This is the perfect business model because there is no wasted costly inventory. Zazzle only stores *blanks* and turns them into products after they have been paid for.

What is your earnings potential of selling online with Zazzle?

When I first started over 10 years ago, I would have never predicted that I could become a millionaire selling on Zazzle, but I did. Ecommerce, as we know it today, was almost non-existent back then. Brick and mortar companies were just starting to open up online stores. Customers were also not comfortable purchasing online and giving out their credit card information to websites they were not sure they could trust. It was definitely a challenge to make money online, back in 2007.

Times have changed, and now selling your art, photography, and graphic designs online, on more than just canvases and posters, is a viable way to run a business and earn a living using your creativity. You just need to use the right ecommerce platform and have access to a proven plan and a mentor.

In fact, if you are not selling online, you are missing out. In 2018, U.S. shoppers spent $125.91 billion online, November 1 to December 31—a 16.5% year-over-year increase from 2017. In 2017, there was a 14.7% increase over the 2016 holiday season, according to Adobe Digital Insights. The numbers and increases are staggering, and you can profit from this boom.

These holiday online sales numbers are just for November and December. However, shoppers are now routinely buying online all year round.

That is why this is the most opportune time in history to be selling online.

Why not everyone is successful on Zazzle, and how you can be

Even though there are over 600,000 designers selling on Zazzle, many people do not know that Zazzle exists, or that it offers this opportunity for creatives to make money online selling through their platform.

When they do find out about it, they give up soon after starting a store because they don't get any sales.

There are also many designers already on Zazzle who are struggling to make the same kind of money that I make. They think you have to struggle for years, like I did, before they can make more than a few hundred dollars. I see their posts on the Zazzle forums all the time. They get frustrated and then angry, and rightly so. However, because of my years of experience and having been where they are on their Zazzle journey, I know what they should be doing to improve their chances to make sales. They are not implementing my 5 steps.

It was not until I put ALL of the 5 steps into action in my Zazzle business that I made a huge leap to 5- and 6-figure earnings results.

Why does implementing The 5 Step Profit Plan™ make all the difference between earning and not earning? It has to do with what we creatives are good at and what we are not. We, as artists, are less comfortable with business, selling and dealing with money. We are blessed with more right brain (creative) abilities than left (logic) brain. Most artists and creatives are extremely talented at what they do, but then they don't know how to monetize their talents. Can you relate?

I have been blessed with both creative and business abilities. That is why I was able to figure out what I needed to do to create my successful Zazzle business. That is how I could put together The 5 Step Profit Plan™, and that is why other creatives using the 5 steps in their Zazzle business are now seeing success.

Because I struggled...

Because I see other creatives, even more talented than I am, struggle...

I have dedicated my life to helping you by taking the struggle out of growing rich and being creative online on Zazzle.

Over the years, I have helped thousands of creatives, just like you, to improve their earnings on Zazzle, using The 5 Step Profit Plan™.

Do you want to know how I can help you get started quickly, or to improve your existing Zazzle business? You can contact me for a private consultation, at support@elkeclarke.com. I would love to chat with you and find out how I can help you.

Elke's Secret to Success

Zazzle is the best ecommerce platform, to create online and grow rich, if you have the right plan of action and mentor.

Summary

In this chapter, you learned that you need the right ecommerce platform (Zazzle), a proven plan to follow to be profitable (The 5 Step Profit Plan™), and a mentor who has already achieved what you want to achieve (me, a million-dollar Zazzle earner).

In Chapter 4, I will show you how to easily get started on Zazzle. Plus, I will tell you what you must do to get noticed, and what mistakes you should avoid making.

Notes:

Chapter 4:

How to Get Started Right Now on Zazzle

"The greatest adventure is what lies ahead." – J. R. R. Tolkien

Open your Zazzle account in less than a minute.

Go to the Zazzle.com website, and create an account.

When you sign up for your Zazzle account, use your best email. Use the email that you use regularly and have frequent access to, because it will be your username and the way Zazzle will communicate with you.

That's it.

You can browse around your account tabs and realize you have been assigned an *associate* number. That is your Zazzle ID. It is important for your payment information and is your affiliate number as well. I will tell you more about that later.

Open up your first virtual store on Zazzle

To sell products and earn royalties from those products, you will need to post them in the virtual store you set up on Zazzle.

Your store name will be how customers find you on the Zazzle website. You will receive your own unique URL (www.zazzle.com/yourstorename), and your store name will be shown next to each product, showcasing you as the designer.

Find the option to open your first store, on your user dashboard, when you are logged into your Zazzle account.

The steps are easy to follow.

The difficult part is naming your store for future success. This takes some thought on your part, and the next few paragraphs will guide you in making your decision.

Choosing a popular niche

Before choosing a store name, you may be wondering which niches sell well and which one you should focus on to maximize sales. This can be daunting, so I have created a free, downloadable cheat sheet for you: *How to Find the Perfect Niche for Your Zazzle Business.* You can find this free bonus gift from me, at **www.CreateOnlineAndGrowRich.com**.

Choose a professional store name

Once you have chosen your niche, it is time to choose a name for your store. Choose your store name wisely because it cannot be changed once you create it. Your store name becomes part of the permanent Zazzle URL for your store. You can edit the store name that is visible in the Zazzle

Marketplace, but the URL can never be changed. This makes it suboptimal for your future business growth if it is not consistent with the rest of your brand across other platforms, like social media and your website.

Consider the following points before you finalize the name for your Zazzle store.

Your Zazzle store name should reflect the content you will be putting in your store, so that there is consistency between what you offer and your name or brand. For example, if you plan on only selling Christmas items, then you might decide on the name, *Christmas Boutique*. You can also choose to have a name that is less product or theme specific, such as *Pretty Paper Goods*, or *BG Design Studio*. However, definitely avoid weird names, like *mike1234*, which makes your store look unprofessional.

Make sure your store name can accommodate future expansion. If your designs are popular, you may want to expand to other print on demand sites, or develop your own website later, and sell your brand on a larger scale.

Ensure your chosen Zazzle store name is available for use

Before choosing a name, check online to see if other companies are already using the name. Obviously, you would not choose a name that was already well known. You want your name to be unique so that you can build your business even beyond Zazzle in the future.

Also, check if your chosen name brings up any negative or unwanted Google search results other than your intended purpose. If your store name search resulted in search results that were totally different than your niche or theme, or were inappropriate, then choose a different name.

Your store name may also have unintended meanings in foreign languages, which can cause you issues in the future. Zazzle sells internationally, so you want to have a name that is acceptable in all languages.

Don't violate copyright laws when choosing a store name

Ensure you are not infringing on existing company trademarks.

In the United States, you can search the TESS copyright and trademark database to find out if your store name has been registered and is off limits. The link to the site is shown below.

https://www.uspto.gov/trademark

An online search in Google will direct you to similar databases, like TESS, for any other country in the world you desire to search for trademarks and copyright.

It is your responsibility to ensure you can legally use a name for your Zazzle store.

Even if it is available on Zazzle as a store name option, you must ensure that you are not violating copyright law. Zazzle's only criteria for accepting the name is that it is available in their database. It does not do a copyright search for you.

TAKE ACTION:
Do you already have a Zazzle store name picked out? Did you check it against the TESS data base?
(https://www.uspto.gov/trademark)

In the "Notes" section in this chapter, I want you to brainstorm and write down your store name ideas in a list, one under the other. Then, beside each name, give it a checkmark if:

a. it's not copyrighted
b. it does not have a negative meaning in a foreign language
c. it suits what you have in mind to post in your store for sale

If you have 3 checkmarks next to your store name, then you are ready to add it into the section on Zazzle where it asks for the name of your store.

Hit ENTER!

If Zazzle says that name is available, then you just opened your Zazzle store.

Congratulations!

What if you have just realized you have the wrong store name to be successful?

If you've been a Zazzle designer for a while, and you just realized from reading this chapter that you are stuck with an ill-chosen name, like mike1234, for your Zazzle store, then you are most likely wondering... "What is my best strategy?"

Unfortunately, the answer is never the same for any of my mentoring students that I have helped with this dilemma. Each case is unique and depends on many factors, all of which are too complex to dive into here in this book. But it is extremely important to resolve this issue in order to improve your overall branding, which is key to the success of your business.

I cover this in great detail in The 5 Step Profit Plan VIP Mentoring Program™. You can find out more details about how to enroll in the program, at the link below.

https://elkeclarke.com/profit/

Elke's Secret to Success

Treat your Zazzle store as a business right from the start. Choose the right Zazzle store name, and get set up properly.

When people ask me to mentor them, one of the most common reasons why they have problems making money on Zazzle is because they have chosen the wrong store name and are not focused on a niche(s). Avoid all the hassles and lack of success that come with a bad Zazzle store name and lack of focus, by choosing your name wisely and designing with purpose.

Post your first virtual product for sale

Making your first product, and posting it for sale on Zazzle, is easy. Choose one of thousands of product types to design on, and then use Zazzle's design tool right on their website to create your design. You can use the tool to add text, images, and shapes to create your unique designs.

Once your design is ready, follow the easy prompts to post your product for sale in your virtual store. The product will also be visible in the Zazzle marketplace, for customers to find, using keyword searches.

TAKE ACTION:
Go ahead! Make your first product by using the Zazzle design tool and adding some text. Create a saying or personalize it with a name or initial. Or upload an image of your artwork or photography or graphic design. Easy! Right?

Follow the steps when prompted, and you will have posted your first product for sale.

In the "Notes" section in this chapter, I want you to write, "I DID IT AND IT WAS EASY!"
Congratulations! You opened up your Zazzle store, and you posted your first product for sale.

What do you do next to make money on Zazzle?

You have just experienced how easy it is to post a product for sale on Zazzle. But now you have realized that there is a lot more to this than just randomly posting products for sale.

I'm certain that you now have a lot of questions:

- What designs can I post that will sell?
- Where can I get images and graphics to use if I don't have any of my own?
- What the heck is copyright, and what do I need to do?
- How many products do I have to post before I make a sale?
- What % royalty should I set?
- How will my products be found so people can buy them?
- Elke, what best practices do you follow to be so successful on Zazzle?

Keep reading, because I answer all these questions, and others you didn't even know you needed to ask. You will have a really good idea on what you need to do, by the end of this chapter.

Images and graphic designs – Use your own, license them for commercial use, or use public domain options

If you are a photographer, artist, or graphic designer, then you can add images of your work onto any Zazzle product and post it for sale. Zazzle's design tool is also extremely robust.

You can use it to create designs without even needing any images or graphics.

Play around with the options, and you will quickly see that it has many amazing features that give you unlimited opportunities to make designs and post them for sale.

What to do if you want to sell photography, art, or graphic designs, but don't have any of your own

If you want to make money on Zazzle, but you don't have your own creative works to choose from, then there are lots of free resources available online to help you get started creating graphics and designs, and then adding the designs to products you post for sale on Zazzle. See further down for a list of some options I use.

You can also find images and graphics that are in the *public domain* and use those. Keep reading further into this chapter, where I go into more detail about *public domain* images and where you can find them.

A third option you have is to purchase commercial use licenses, in order to use premade graphics and fonts, or pay people to create graphic designs and artwork for you that you own the copyright to. In either case, you can then add these designs, images, etc. to Zazzle products, and post the products for sale in your Zazzle store.

Fonts – License them or use copyright free options

Zazzle has obtained licenses for hundreds of fonts for commercial use, and has added them to their design tool menu. This is an added bonus for you because you can use these fonts for free, without any additional licensing requirements on your part. You can access these fonts directly while creating your product design in the Zazzle design tool.

Google Fonts is also a great source for free commercial use fonts, and can be found at this link:
https://www.google.com/fonts

If Zazzle does not offer the font in their design tool, and if the font is copyright protected, you will need to purchase a commercial use license. Yes, even fonts, just like photos and graphics, are copyrighted.

Comply with copyright laws

You can make products by adding your own photos or graphic images, as long as they do not violate any copyright laws. It is always up to you, the designer, to have written proof that you have the permission to use any font, digital graphic, photo, or vector file (or any creative work) for commercial use. The following site is a good place to start your search to see if something is trademarked or copyrighted.

https://www.uspto.gov/trademark

Even if it is your own photo, you might not be able to use it if it is of a photo or drawing of a thing, place, or name that is protected under copyright law.

Case Study – Copyright

For example, the Lone Cypress and the Pebble Beach Golf Course in California are copyrighted, so any image of either is not allowed to be sold on Zazzle.

You must do your own due diligence. Zazzle does not have an approval process, so you can put up any design, etc. on a product, and post it for sale. But if a copyright holder contacts Zazzle with a takedown notice, then your products with the copyright infringement, even if they have been up for years and selling, will be deleted. You may even have to pay back your earnings.

Many sellers on Zazzle have been disappointed because products that they listed for sale, with their own photography or painting of the Lone Cypress, have been removed. Even though it was their photograph and their creative painting of the Lone Cypress, it does not matter. If you are seeking commercial gain by using a copyrighted item, then you are at fault, and Zazzle is extremely strict about copyright.

How to use public domain images and where to find them

A public domain image is an image with no copyright protection. It is NOT an image you found online, *on the*

Internet. Your finding the image on the Internet does not mean it is a public domain image. This is a big misconception many people have.

If an image is classified as *public domain use,* then it is *free to use and resell for commercial use.*

Public domain use can happen after the copyright protection runs out on a creative work (font, graphic design, logo, a creation like art and photographs, or things like a book or music, etc.), because a specified number of years (depending on each country's laws) have passed since the item was created. People can renew copyright on items, however. You must double check to see if someone's estate has applied for an extension of copyright.

Rules about how long a creative work is under copyright protection before it becomes part of the *public domain,* are country-specific. Since you are selling on Zazzle, which has international reach, do your homework and make sure you are complying with all international copyright laws.

For *"free for commercial use"* items, it is best to find graphics and images that are classified as *public domain use.*

Always perform due diligence to ensure you are complying with copyright law. Here are a few sites to check out for *"free for commercial use"* images and graphics. Just a word of caution: Even when a site says *public domain images,* you must still do your homework to make sure the site is truly only hosting public domain images and vectors.

Resources for public domain images

Below are links to resources for public domain images, which I have put together for you:

- A great resource for information about public domain image resources –
  https://en.wikipedia.org/wiki/Wikipedia:Public_domain_image_resources

- Clker.com is a free online sharing service, with free public domain vector clipart and photos.

- Pixabay.com is a free source for photos and vector graphics that are published under Creative Commons CC0, which means they are under *public domain use*. Each contributor may have some additional instructions that you must abide by in order to use their photo or vector; so, be informed and comply.

- Morguefile.com is a free source for photos that you can remix and alter for commercial use, as long as you don't sell them in their original form. For photos of people, which you might want to use as a placeholder in your Zazzle product design, you must have proof of a signed model release form.

What are Creative Commons Licenses, and how can you use these to get free images and vectors?

If the creator of the image, graphic, etc. waives some or all of their copyright rights by stating the type of uses that are allowed, then you may be able to use the image even though it is not legally under the public domain yet. That's why you will see notes next to images you find online, indicating what type of Creative Commons designation it is. The following link is a really helpful resource in understanding Creative Commons Licenses.

https://en.wikipedia.org/wiki/Creative_Commons_license

How to create designs or manipulate your images and designs for use on Zazzle products

You can use the easy to use and extremely comprehensive Zazzle design tool to make designs right on the Zazzle platform.

If you want an external software to create graphics or manipulate your images, eventually you will want to upgrade to more advanced tools, such as Adobe Illustrator or Adobe Photoshop, which are paid software programs. But for now, you can use GIMP.

GIMP (GNU Image Manipulation Program) is a free graphic design software alternative to purchasing a graphic design software license. It is a powerful image manipulation program used for photo retouching, image creation, and text layers. This program runs on Windows and Mac systems.

https://www.gimp.org/

Set your own royalty

Unlike other online print-on-demand companies, Zazzle allows designers to set their own royalties above the base price of a product. You can choose a royalty in the range of 5% to 99% higher earnings.

Some products actually sell more at a higher price due to perceived value. You do not always have to set your royalty low in order to get sales.

If you have a unique product or design, which is in high demand, customers will pay a premium price. For premium items on Zazzle, you can set the royalty as high as you desire (up to 99%). It is important to remember that Zazzle attracts many different types of customers, including ones who will pay top dollar for unique and high-quality items.

To be competitive with your pricing for products and designs that are more mainstream, you can compare the prices of similar products, both inside and outside of the Zazzle marketplace, to help you determine what you should set your royalty at for your Zazzle products.

Elke's Secret to Success

Set your royalty in the range of 10 to 15% as a general rule. You can set it higher for unique one-off designs.

Can you make money with a low royalty setting?

Yes! Why do I suggest you set your royalty in the range of 10 to 15% ? Because Zazzle has many promotions, and they select items to promote that are within a specific royalty, usually 10%. I take advantage of this to receive free promotion by Zazzle.

One of the key factors in the success of selling your product designs is the royalty rate setting. Experiment, and keep trying until you find the rate that works for you, based on your niche and what you are offering as designs on the products.

It's a balance of being competitively priced but also knowing you can charge a premium for unique items.

"Even though I do have some items set at a higher royalty rate, I have sold millions of dollars' worth of Zazzle products by setting my royalty rates for between 10 and 15%, which I find to be my sweet spot." – Elke Clarke

Promoting your products

If you don't tell people about your products, how will they know they are for sale? You need to promote your Zazzle products.

You can use social media, websites, blogs, email, YouTube, and more.

Zazzle makes it super simple for you to promote by having social media share buttons right next to the Zazzle product you want to share. If you are logged in to both your social media platform and your Zazzle account, then when you click on one of the social media icons on the Zazzle product page, your link and your referral code (more on that below) will automatically be generated and be posted on the social media site.

Setting up any social media account is free, so take advantage of this and make accounts up with your Zazzle store name. You should create accounts on Facebook, Twitter, and Pinterest, because Zazzle has convenient sharing buttons for each of these.

For any other platforms, Zazzle has this convenient chain link button, which, when you click it, will give you a popup window where you can copy your unique code and use it to create hyperlinks.

Promoting your products has 2 benefits:

- Your products will be seen on these social media platforms, driving traffic back to your Zazzle store and products, increasing your chance of sales

- Your link will have your unique Zazzle ID referral code embedded in it. This means that if a customer uses your link to get to Zazzle, and buys anything on Zazzle, you will receive a 15% affiliate commission as part of the Zazzle Associate Program.

You can earn 15% affiliate income by promoting Zazzle

By signing up for a Zazzle account, you automatically became an *associate* (affiliate) of Zazzle. That means, when you share a link from Zazzle to your social media platforms, website, blog, or through email, and the customer clicks on your link to buy anything on Zazzle, you earn 15% of anything they buy.

This is called referral income, and you receive this on top of any royalty % you set, if the customer bought your own product on Zazzle.

This is a fantastic way to double your income from the sale of your product. It would depend on the royalty you have set, but you can do the math and see the potential.

Plus, if you are better at promoting than designing, you can earn 15% if you promote and link back to ANY product or landing page on Zazzle, not just your own.

Think of the potential. You can promote all the brand names and top sellers on Zazzle without ever having to design anything or do any work on creating popular products yourself.

Zazzle's affiliate program is a viable second option you have to make money online using Zazzle.

Plan ahead to get the most sales of seasonal products

Do you ever wonder why summer clothes are in the stores in February, or Easter products are in the stores the day after Valentine's Day?

It is the nature of the sales cycle, and is something you need to account for when making products geared towards a particular seasonal niche on Zazzle.

You need to have your products available for sale at a time when customers are buying for that season. If people start buying for Christmas in October, then your products should be made in September.

Also, consider that your products need to be available for marketers and promoters to create marketing materials well before a particular purchasing season begins.

That means your Christmas products should be posted for sale by August or September.

Elke's Secret to Success

The general rule of thumb is to post for sale your seasonal products, 2 to 3 months before a seasonal event.

Celebrate when you make your first sale.

Whether you make 29 cents, like I did, or more on your first sale, you must celebrate.

Why? Because look how far I have come after I made my first sale!

When I made my 29-cent sale, I celebrated the heck out of this small sale because I saw the future potential.

I believed that Zazzle would be THE WAY for me to create my dream life.

You can read more about my story, at
https://www.elkeclarke.com/about.

When you receive that first email from Zazzle, telling you that you made a sale, jump up and down. Shout out loud. Do your happy dance!

Now you know you are on your way. Yes, it will be hard work, but now you have proof that you can make money on Zazzle. You just need to do more of the same to increase your earnings.

Celebrate and relish the moment. Take in all the good feelings you are experiencing of succeeding, and build on them to keep you motivated to keep growing your Zazzle business.

Realize you are on a new journey, which has the potential to change your life as you now know it.

Keep striving to reach your financial goals.

I know you've got this.

Receive your Zazzle payments monthly

After you follow the instructions on how to set up your payment information on Zazzle, you will be paid monthly on the 15th.

Your royalties owed to you will be cleared 30 days after they were earned, and will be paid out on the next pay period.

Referrals and Volume Bonus earnings follow the same criteria.

You can read all the fine print as to how it all works, once you sign up for a Zazzle account.

Treat it as a business right from the start

If you want to earn a realistic, consistent income, month after month, from your Zazzle store, you will need to treat it as a business right from the start. I have practiced that advice, and it has paid off for me. I have sold over 10 million dollars' worth of Zazzle products by following my *10 Best Zazzle Business Practices.*

Elke's 10 Best Zazzle Business Practices:

1. Be professional. Presenting your store and your profile in a professional manner to your customers will create customer confidence and help build your brand recognition.

2. Put in the time. It takes time and hard work to create something that is successful. Don't give up. It is important to remember to be patient and consistent with creating new products and promoting them.

3. Have earnings goals. Set goals for your monthly and yearly earnings. Review your progress, and make changes based on your monthly sales data.

4. Don't take it personally. If you are an artist, a photographer, or a graphic designer, and you are upset that no one is buying your amazing creation, you MUST move on. If your close-up photo of a golf ball on a cell phone case sells more than a stretched canvas print of your best artistic photo of a golf course in the morning light, then go with what sells. Your goal is to sell on Zazzle, not to win a prize for your artistic work. To be recognized for your artistic abilities, you can enter a photo competition.

5. Expand your product line to avoid missed opportunities. If you have a design on one product that sells well, make sure to add the same design to other items. If you have a popular business card, make the matching business card holder or matching letterhead.

6. Manage your time effectively. Make lists and set objectives for product creation and promotion. Then schedule time in your calendar to break the jobs down into manageable tasks.

7. Invest a portion of your earnings. Once you make money on Zazzle, invest a portion of your earnings back into your company to improve your earning capabilities. License some graphics to use in your designs, upgrade your graphics software, or buy a better computer.

8. Upgrade your skills. As you grow your business, you will need to keep up to date with new developments in software and trends and techniques. Many free tutorials are online. Set some time aside on a regular basis to learn something new.

9. Make a backup. Back up your digital copies of your designs, graphics, photos, and programs, using an online backup service or an external hard drive. Your designs that you add onto products on Zazzle are your copyrighted designs and your property. It is important to keep a record.

10. Give back. When you give back, the rewards are always many, and sometimes unexpected. Give your time and expertise by getting involved in the Zazzle forum, or use some of your profits to support a cause you feel strongly about. If

you are not certain where to provide support, participate in Zazzle's charity initiatives,
such as disaster relief.

Are you ready to grow your Zazzle business?

Now that you have started on Zazzle, and you have set up the basics, you might be thinking, "How do I grow my Zazzle business?"

I created a free quiz to help you define and clarify the direction and scope of your Zazzle business. This quiz also has a special link to free resources that you can access. You will find these invaluable as you dive deeper into setting up your Zazzle business. Go to the following link to access the quiz.

https://www.CreateOnlineAndGrowRich.com

TAKE ACTION:
This chapter was full of action steps for you. Take a moment to go back through this chapter to ensure that you have completed each one.

In the "Notes" section in this chapter, I want you to write down each of the sections you completed, and promise yourself to complete any that you missed. Congratulations on your accomplishments.

Elke's Secret to Success

Treat it as a business right from the start. Do the planning for long-term success. Choose the right niche, store name, and avoid copyright issues.

Summary

In this chapter, you learned how to open up your Zazzle account, set up your first Zazzle store, make your first product, and how and when you can get paid. I have also given you many crucial tips and guidelines for success that I use to be successful on Zazzle, including **my 10 Best Zazzle Business Practices**. With this information, you can start your Zazzle business and slowly build up your earnings.

But to ramp up your Zazzle business to the 5 and 6-figure level, you need to follow a proven plan and get guidance from a mentor (someone who has already accomplished what you want to accomplish). In the next chapter, I can't wait to share with you my proven plan that I follow: The 5 Step Profit Plan™. It is the reason for my multi-million-dollar success on Zazzle.

Notes:

Chapter 5:

Ramping up Your Zazzle Business to Millionaire Status

"Money is multiplied in practical value depending on the number of W's you control in your life: what you do, when you do it, where you do it, and with whom you do it."

– Timothy Ferriss, author of *The 4-Hour Workweek*

In this chapter, you will learn what it takes to grow your Zazzle business to the 6 and 7-figures.

Your financial success will be greater, the more you make the right choices for the 4 W's:

- what you do (the right plan of action)
- with whom you do it (the right mentor)
- where you do it (the right place to make money)
- when you do it (the right choice to take massive action, immediately and daily)

The 4 W's

#1 – What you do

Follow a proven plan that has worked for others who have achieved what you want to achieve. The 5 Step Profit Plan™ is my proven plan that I created and have followed to build my multi-million-dollar Zazzle business. The members in The 5 Step Profit Plan VIP Mentoring Program™ are successful because they also follow The 5 Step Profit Plan™, and they have me as their mentor.

#2 – When you do it

The time to take action is now, especially if you have a proven plan. After you start, you must take consistent action every day to move forward. Zazzle is not a get-rich- quick scheme. You need to do the work to put The 5 Step Profit Plan™ into place. Once you have your Zazzle business running the way you want, then you can enjoy the time freedom and financial freedom you dream about. However, in the beginning, it is important to work a minimum of 20 hours a week to implement The 5 Step Profit Plan™.

The key to success is the consistent act of doing the right things. Do you have a lot of knowledge but find it difficult to get started? That is why the members of my 5 Step Profit Plan VIP Mentoring Program™ are so successful—the program tells you when to do what. You follow the steps and take purposeful action daily. Plus, my mentoring program keeps you motivated to take action consistently.

#3 – Where you do it

You can choose to try to figure out on your own which print on demand companies work for you, but you would be wasting your valuable time. Instead, learn from my experience and choose Zazzle, the best print on demand company. You can also consider selling on Etsy, Amazon, or Shopify, but these companies require more work and investment dollars for you to succeed.

Zazzle is the best print on demand company for product selection, royalty and earning potential, ease of use, innovation, and worldwide expansion. Plus, Zazzle is better than Shopify, Etsy, or Amazon, because there are no upfront costs, no fees, no sales quotas, no restrictions, no production of products, no time wasted on fulfilling orders, no dealing with customers, no dealing with shipping, no costs for supplies and shipping, and more. The sooner you focus your efforts on the one platform that will give you the most benefits, the sooner you will gain your profits.

#4 – With whom you do it

If you want to become a professional baseball player, or learn how to dance, or get into shape, you get a coach, teacher, or trainer. If you want to build a business or improve your life, then you need the help of a mentor or personal coach: a mentor or coach who has already accomplished what you want to achieve; a mentor or coach who can guide you, motivate you, and support you. Your success depends on choosing the right person to mentor and coach you.

"A mentor is someone who allows you to see the hope inside yourself." – Oprah Winfrey

My struggles and how I overcame them

When I first started out, I didn't have the 4W's in place. I was driven, and worked hard every day to make money online.

Can you relate to this?

I was definitely following the *when*, but I wasn't following a proven plan (the *what*), so my efforts were not targeted to accomplishing the right goals that would result in long-term success. I also had not found the right platform (the *where*), and I definitely did not have a mentor to show me the way (*with whom*).

Over time, through trial and error, I started to get the 4W's in place. I found and focused on Zazzle, the right place to make money (the *where*). I developed and perfected my 5 Step Profit Plan™ to consistently generate significant income (the *what*). I was more effective in getting results because I was consistently taking the right actions (the *when*).

However, I never found a Zazzle mentor (the *with whom*). **It is the reason why it took me so long to achieve results when I first started on Zazzle.** If I would have had a Zazzle mentor, I would not have wasted so much time and made so many mistakes figuring things out by my myself.

That is why I have dedicated my life to mentoring you.

You are reading this book because you want to be successful online, but you definitely don't want to take as long as I did to reach your goals. Am I correct? That is why you need to choose the best ecommerce platform, the proven plan of action, and the right mentor to speed up your journey to online success.

"One of the greatest values of mentors is the ability to see ahead what others cannot see, and to help them navigate a course to their destination." – John C. Maxwell

My Story

I desperately wanted to prove that I could grow rich using my creativity. All my life, I was told by loved ones and authority figures that I can't make money being creative. They would say to me: *"You can't make money being creative. That's why there is the phrase, "Starving Artist." When are you going to get a real job? Art is a hobby."* Ouch! Maybe you have had the same experience.

Because of these negative influences, I suppressed my creativity and got a job in *the real world*. I quickly realized I was going to be working extremely hard for a long time, and going more and more into debt rather than growing rich like I wanted. Plus, I was miserable because I was not being creative.

But all that changed when ecommerce companies like Zazzle popped up on the Internet about 10 years ago. All the barriers to traditional ways to make money as a creative were torn down, and new opportunities were created. It gave me (and now you) the opportunity to do what I love and to grow rich.

TAKE ACTION:
First, write in the "Notes" section at the end of this chapter, what has stopped you from using your creativity to grow rich. Is it the misguided messages you have received from people, whose opinions you value? Is it the fact that you did not know about Zazzle?

Second, write down how you feel, now that you have found a way to be creative and earn money. Take some time to let it sink in that you can do this. You can make it happen for yourself. Write down, "I can grow rich using my creativity!"

My story continued...

When I first started making money on Zazzle, I was just happy that I could use my earnings to treat my family to something small, like a night at the movies, or save up for a vacation.

Then, when I started making more money on Zazzle, I realized I could have a bigger impact on my own life and my family's life. I used my Zazzle earnings to pay off the mortgage on our house, put my kids through school, and much more.

At one point, there was this switch in my mindset. Instead of just focusing on making money to pay the bills and buy things, I realized that I was running a proper business, which was generating some serious yearly sales numbers.

My success wasn't just the fact that I was making over $100,000 a year so that I could use the money to pay for things.

It was the realization that I was selling over 1 million dollars' worth of products on Zazzle each year, that really hit home with me.

"I had created a hugely successful 7-figure business, selling my creativity, using Zazzle as my ecommerce platform!"

Now it is your turn

As you can see from my story, it is a slow but steady growth business. Zazzle is not a get-rich-quick scheme. It is an investment in your future, and it grows steadily if done right. But once it is established, it is powerful and can serve you in many ways.

To start investing in your future, start growing your Zazzle business today.

You own the copyright to your designs on Zazzle, and they can continue selling for you for a long time after you have posted them for sale. I still sell products I posted 10 years ago. Can you imagine doing 5 minutes of work, 10 years ago, and still making money from it? Then multiply that by the number of products you have on Zazzle that sell. You can see how your sales can easily snowball to generate larger and larger sales totals.

Your Zazzle business is your property, which can be inherited. Imagine your children or grandchildren inheriting your business that continues to generate passive income for years to come.

You can also sell your Zazzle business to an investor. Imagine selling your Zazzle business for a huge sum of money. Your business is valuable because your investor realizes that even if they don't do any more work on your business, the passive income from it can generate a greater return on their investment than other financial investments!

TAKE ACTION:

So, how do you get started fast on your journey to grow rich using your creativity? You need to put the 4 W's in place. You need the *what* (the right proven plan), the *where* (Zazzle), the *when* (your commitment to taking massive action consistently and daily – I know you've got this), and the *with whom* (the right mentor).

In the "Notes" section at the end of this chapter, make a small 2-column table. Write down the 4 W's underneath each other in the left column. Then, in the right column, for each line of text, add what you will use to put the 4 W's into action. (For example, "where" = "Zazzle")

You've got the drive and determination

Congratulations! You are already on your way to growing rich using your creativity because you have the drive, determination, and commitment (otherwise, you wouldn't be reading this book). You have had the dream of starting your own business for as long as you can remember. Or you work on your side hustle, wishing and hoping it would finally make the money you need to quit your 9 to 5 job.

You are not alone. Millions of people around the world work hard every day to get ahead.

The reason people are stuck and don't achieve their dream goals is that they are only doing what they know.

You will never get ahead if you do not learn new things, learn how to do them properly, and have someone to guide you who knows what to do to achieve the results you want.

You have the opportunity to get unstuck by following the advice in this book.

"If I have seen further, it is by standing on the shoulders of giants." – Isaac Newton

Use the proven plan of action – The 5 Step Profit Plan™

How did I go from earning 29 cents on my first sale, to earning over 1 million dollars on Zazzle? I developed my proven plan because I learned from my many struggles and failures over time. Once I was achieving success, I realized I was following 5 steps consistently. If I stopped doing one of these steps, I saw a decrease in sales.

It was clear that I had to follow all 5 steps together, at the same time, consistently, over time. Following all 5 steps, as I built my Zazzle business, is what brought me to my million-dollar earnings result.

As my business grew, and I became known as the authority on Zazzle, I began to mentor people who wanted to know my secrets on how to easily sell on Zazzle. I took the 5 steps, which I was following for myself, and formalized them into a proven plan of action that you can follow and get results like I did. (*I must make sure you understand that I cannot make any income claim statements. Your success depends on your efforts to implement The 5 Step Profit Plan™ effectively. That being said, many of my students have seen dramatic increases in their earnings.*)

That's how I came up with The 5 Step Profit Plan™. Fast forward to today, and hundreds of people have used The 5 Step Profit Plan™ to sell more on Zazzle. The people I have taught and mentored come from all different kinds of situations.

Some have never even heard of Zazzle, and used the program to start from scratch. Others have been on Zazzle but were not achieving their earnings goals. The backgrounds and skill sets vary as well. Some are artists, photographers, graphic designers, or just creative. Others have no background in design at all, but they use solutions to get what they need to run a successful Zazzle business.

Even though my program members come from different backgrounds, skill sets, etc., they all see the potential of Zazzle, and want to use it to grow rich so they can enjoy time freedom and do what they love.

The 5 steps of The 5 Step Profit Plan™ explained

It's time to describe each of the 5 steps in detail. I will list them and then go into more detail for each one.

STEP 1: Proper Set Up
STEP 2: Goals and Mindset
STEP 3: Production
STEP 4: Promotion
STEP 5: Analysis and Implementation

As simple as the 5 steps seem, there is much depth and complexity to each one. Implementing the nuisances of the 5 steps correctly, makes all the difference in the degree of success you experience.

The 5 Step Profit Plan™ is a business plan for achieving success on the Zazzle ecommerce platform. The plan incorporates the best practices of other successful businesses and applies them to the Zazzle business model.

STEP 1: Proper Setup

You must first lay down a solid foundation on which to build your Zazzle business. There are 2 components to proper setup. First, you must set up your Zazzle store correctly in order to look professional and organized, so that customers can find what they are looking to buy. Second, you must train yourself to design with the customer in mind, and label your products properly in order that customers can find and purchase them. There is much more to STEP 1, but this is the essence of what you need to achieve in order to complete STEP 1.

Chapter 4 covers many of the key action steps you need to take to complete STEP 1. The rest of STEP 1 cannot be taught in a book. It can only be shown to you with step-by-step video training.

That is why I created **The 5 Step Profit Plan Program™**. The program makes it fun and easy to get your Zazzle store set up properly. It takes you right from the beginning, opening up your account and creating your first store, to posting your first product for sale. It also trains you how to make and post for sale the 25 most popular product types that sell well on Zazzle. As well, you are taught how to make the most popular design templates that consistently sell well on Zazzle. These training videos take care of the rest of what you need to do to complete STEP 1.

STEP 2: Goals and Mindset

Goals

You must set the right goals, both short-term and long-term, in order to grow your business to the 6 and 7-figure level. Your goals should include financial goals, as well as milestones you want to achieve for every aspect of running your business. To reach your goals, you must also hold yourself accountable and take specific and targeted action to continually experience progress and growth.

Setting goals and achieving them is not easy to do successfully. How many times have you ambitiously set goals and then proceeded to let the deadline slip by, or push back the date you were to start something; or worse yet, make excuses that let you off the hook for not sticking to your plans to get things done. I've done it and will continue to do it. I am sure you have and will do so in the future too. We are all human. The secret is to get the help you need by using certain techniques, as well as being accountable to a mentor to stay on track.

Another big issue is knowing what the goals should be to end up achieving where you want to go. I know just how difficult it is to set goals and accomplish them. That is why I have devoted several chapters in this book, including Chapters 6 and 10, to helping you set your goals and stay committed to them.

My mentoring program takes goal setting and achieving your goals to the next level, beyond what I can do for you in this book. I guide you in your goal setting, using my 10 years of experience on what it takes and what you need to do to keep growing your Zazzle business. Then I motivate you and keep you committed to reach those goals.

Belief Mindset

The right mindset is also key to your success. From my experience with my students, I have found that they do not even hear, see, or comprehend properly what I teach them until they are in the right mindset.

If you are in the wrong headspace, you cannot fully comprehend the instructions and carry them out in a manner that leads to the growth and success of your business.

Mindset can affect all aspects of how you run your business. Since you are a solo entrepreneur, you have no one else to make you aware of your mindset blocks. You think you are doing great, but you are actually hindering your own success because of your mindset.

However, through my mentoring, my students understood that their mindset was holding them back from achieving their goals and true potential. For example, they were doing things such as setting their goals too low or too high, procrastinating, doing busy work, and avoiding doing crucial actions that would grow their business. They were not seeing opportunities that were right in front of them, and they were thinking on a small scale rather than one that would bring them to the higher income level.

"A mentor is someone who sees more talent and ability within you than you see in yourself, and helps bring it out of you." – Bob Proctor

Money Mindset

You must have a healthy relationship with money. If you do not, then you must address this money mindset before you can achieve your full potential to grow your business to the 6 and 7-figure level. You cannot be successful if you have the wrong ideas and values about money, how people create wealth, and what it means to have wealth. Your belief about whether you deserve wealth and have the ability to do the tasks required to achieve it are also huge mindset shifts that you must make before you can move forward and take the actions required to grow your business.

Mindset is so important that I am devoting Chapters 7 and 8 to it in this book. Do not dismiss it as fluff or think you are OK and can just do it. Many of my students have benefited from taking the time to deal with their mindset blocks. They have good intentions, are wonderful people, have amazing talent, and want to be successful with all their heart and soul, and yet they had mindset blocks which were holding them back from reaching their full potential on Zazzle.

STEP 3: Production

Production is all about creating products for sale in your virtual store. It's a simple and obvious concept, and yet is so complex. You will not make substantial money by putting up just any design on any product, and flooding the marketplace with thousands of products that consumers do not want to buy. Instead, you must design for popular niches and provide relevant designs that customers are interested in purchasing.

Whether you are an artist, photographer, graphic designer, or just like to create, you can make sales on Zazzle. However, the number of sales will depend on how you present your unique designs to the customer, on the product they are looking for. There are thousands of product options that you can add your designs to and post for sale. This creates an incredible selection, and many opportunities for you to use a targeted systematic approach to generate an ever-growing inventory that sells consistently for you in your store, year after year.

Production, when done correctly and with purpose, can be extremely lucrative.

The 5 Step Profit Plan Program™ covers production in extreme detail. You will not only be told what the 25 most popular product types are that sell well on Zazzle, but you will be making them and posting them for sale by following the step-by-step videos. Many students sell products in their first month of being in the program, because I tell you exactly what you need to do to make sales. Plus, you will be taught how to easily create the most popular design templates that consistently sell well on Zazzle. Once you are familiar with these rudimentary skills, you will be taught and prompted to put into action all the other key components of production that are required for massive growth.

STEP 4: Promotion

After posting your products for sale, you may think that sales will just flood in. But in order to make sales, customers need to be able to find your products. That's why promotion plays such a crucial role in the sales process.

What forms of promotion can you use to get the word out about your amazing products? Pinterest, Instagram, Facebook, and Twitter are great places for you to promote your products. Zazzle makes it easy for you with promotion buttons right on their website. You can also use YouTube, blogs, your website, forums, email, word of mouth, podcasts, and any other creative ways to get your message out about your products and your Zazzle business.

Getting your products and your brand message (for more on brand, see Chapter 9) out into the world, through promotion, is essential for the rapid growth of your business.

Social media changes so frequently that it would not be justified to provide you with specific details here in the book on how to promote effectively on each platform. Instead, check out www.elkeclarke.com/blog for recent articles related to promotion.

Effective promotion also creates more revenue for you, because you earn 15% referral income in addition to your sales (royalty) income when you bring a customer to Zazzle to purchase your product. You earn this referral (or affiliate) income even if the customer buys a different product on Zazzle than the one you promoted. That means you have the potential to multiply your total income from Zazzle, using a second income stream.

STEP 5: Analysis and Implementation

If you don't like numbers, then you may think you can skip this step, but it too is crucial to the growth of your business. You must complete STEP 5. Zazzle provides you with your sales and income data, which you can then use to do specific analysis to see your progress. Based on your results, you can then decide whether to continue or discontinue doing certain actions to grow your business. Then you must implement your new plan of action.

This analysis must be done regularly so you can act on the results quickly and effectively. This will drive your business forward. If you wait or put it off, you will not be in control of your business. Without control, you will not be able to achieve 6 and 7-figure growth.

Unfortunately, STEP 5 is difficult to do without a mentor, a mentor who has had years of experience and success troubleshooting. However, doing STEP 5 properly is directly related to the speed in which your business grows. Many of my students, in the mentoring program, see exponential growth in their Zazzle business once they take advantage of my guidance with the analysis and implementation step.

How you can create predictable passive income

When I use The 5 Step Profit Plan™ in my Zazzle business, it creates the perfect passive income model. After I built my business to the level I wanted, I began to work less and less, while my Zazzle business began to work for me more and more. My goal was to sell at least 1 million dollars' worth of products each year, which would provide me with the 100K income. I needed to enjoy life and not work more than a few hours a week. I was inspired by Timothy Ferriss, author of *The 4-Hour Workweek.* I accomplished my goal, using The 5 Step Profit Plan™ in my Zazzle business.

My predictable income has given me the TIME FREEDOM to enjoy precious moments with my family, take month long vacations, and pursue my passions, including my philanthropy initiatives, and empowering and mentoring you to achieve your dream life.

Why is The 5 Step Profit Plan™ timeless, and why does it work?

The 5 Step Profit Plan™ is my secret formula for success on Zazzle. To date, my Zazzle business has generated over 10 million in sales, and the number keeps growing. By the time this book is published, or if you read it later, my numbers will have gone up significantly. I am not bragging or boasting to make you feel uneasy. I am telling you my results, as lofty as they are, with confidence, because of my past experience with the sales in my Zazzle business. The 5 Step Profit Plan™ works so well that it allows me to predict my future income, and I can take specific action steps that I know will work to increase my income if I want.

Would you like to be able to predict your Zazzle income?

The 5 Step Profit Plan™ works consistently, even when massive and inevitable changes occur on Zazzle. Changes occur rapidly and frequently in the ecommerce space, and Zazzle is no exception. In fact, Zazzle is such a great ecommerce platform because it continues to innovate and change to keep at the forefront of the online buying experience for customers.

The 5 Step Profit Plan™ prepares you for these changes and shows you how to alter your course of action, and to adapt once a change happens. That means your business will be insulated from the full force of the change, and you will feel empowered to adapt, and to know what alterations to make quickly to minimize the impact on your Zazzle business, as well as maximize your profitability.

To help you easily understand The 5 Step Profit Plan™, and quickly implement the STEPS, I have created **The 5 Step Profit Plan VIP Mentoring Program™.** You can find more information about it on my website, at https://elke clarke.com/profit/.

Invest in yourself

"Personal development is a major time-saver. The better you become, the less time it takes you to achieve your goals." – Brian Tracy

It's clear that you are committed to the success of your online business. After reading this far in the book, you have also made the decision to use Zazzle to grow rich. So now you just need to be mentored by the Zazzle mentor who has achieved what you want to achieve, and use the proven Zazzle plan that worked for your mentor.

It is at this stage that your brain plays tricks on you. It sends you conflicting messages. On the one hand, you totally agree that you need the help of a mentor and a program to see results quicker than you would achieve on your own. On the other hand, since you are starting what you perceive to be a *small business* or *side hustle*, you think it is too small to invest in right now, and that you can do it on your own.

But you need to think big. This is not your hobby. It is supposed to generate enough money for you to quit your 9 to 5 job. This business will pay for your retirement and give you the time freedom to do the things you love. It means your business needs to be a proper business. Think big, and get the help you need to build your business, so that it grows more rapidly and creates the long-term passive income stream you desire.

If you wanted to drive a car to the grocery store, would you invent the wheel first? No! You would get in your car, a proven way to get to the store, and drive there with confidence, arriving in the fastest time possible. Was it a good investment for you to buy an expensive car? Yes!

Case Study – Brandon invested in himself and increased sales 2,000%

"Investing in yourself is the best investment you will ever make. It will not only improve your life, it will improve the lives of all those around you." – Robin Sharma

Brandon loves being a photographer but works at a corporate job to pay the bills. He was aware of Zazzle and was convinced that it was a great way to make money online with his photography and graphic design skills. But he just wasn't making the money he wanted. He struggled on his own for over 5 years!

When I opened enrollment in The 5 Step Profit Plan VIP Mentoring Program™ for the first time, Brandon did not hesitate. He invested in himself by signing up. He could have made numerous excuses—"I can't afford it; I am too busy with my job; I can do it myself;" and more—but he took action instead. He was one of the first people to enroll in my mentoring program.

Investing in himself has really paid off for Brandon. In 18 months, he has sold over $250,000 US of Zazzle products. He is on track to reach $400,000 in sales in 2 years. Why? **Because his Zazzle products are generating passive**

income for him. He made these products over the past year, and now they sell over and over again.

The *work once, earn often* business model

The products Brandon made in the past are selling repeatedly without any additional effort on his part. Every day, he can focus on posting more products for sale in his Zazzle store, which will add to his earnings, making his projected sales increase even more.

Brandon experienced a huge shift in his ability to grow rich, because he invested in himself.

You are your own company. It is up to you to create your wealth. That is why you need to invest in yourself, so that you can become the person who is capable of building your successful online business.

Before Brandon invested in himself, he struggled to sell anything on Zazzle, and his business was failing. After he invested in himself, within a short time period, he experienced a 2,000% increase in sales. Now his business is growing and creating wealth for him.

You can read about Brandon's first year in the program, in these 2 articles.

https://elkeclarke.com/how-to-sell-on-zazzle-a-zazzle-success-story-part-1/

https://elkeclarke.com/how-to-sell-on-zazzle-a-zazzle-success-story-part-2/

The 5 Step Profit Plan™ is the business plan you can use to achieve success on the Zazzle ecommerce platform. The plan incorporates the best practices of successful businesses and applies them to the Zazzle business model.

To help you easily understand The 5 Step Profit Plan™, and quickly implement the STEPS, I have created The 5 Step Profit Plan VIP Mentoring Program™. For more information, visit my website at https://www.elke clarke.com/profit/.

Elke's Secret to Success

You can dream big, but to actually grow rich, you need to have the drive and determination to succeed, the proven profit plan to follow, and a successful mentor to guide and support you.

Summary

In this chapter, you learned exactly what you can do to grow rich with your creativity.

Follow a proven plan. Listen to the guidance of a qualified mentor. Choose the right revenue generating ecommerce platform. Take targeted action, today and daily, from now on.

From the case studies that you read about, you know that Zazzle is a great ecommerce platform, but it is difficult to earn a substantial income unless you build your business properly by implementing all 5 steps of The 5 Step Profit Plan™. The proven plan and the continual mentoring are the keys to success on Zazzle.

In Chapter 5, I gave you many action steps that you can take to begin implementing (STEP 1) (Proper Setup). In Chapter 6, I will cover goal setting (STEP 2) and give you valuable tips so that you can accomplish your goals on your journey to grow rich with your creativity.

Notes:

Chapter 6:

Be Awesome at Goal Setting to Succeed

"Make each day count by setting specific goals to succeed, then putting forth every effort to exceed your own expectations." – Les Brown

You set goals all the time. You might set them formally by writing them down and making plans. Most likely, you also just say things like, "I should do that," or, "I want to do that." That's goal setting too, on a more casual level. Either way, how you set your goals, and what you set as goals, affects whether or not you will actually achieve them.

Right now, when you set goals, how many of these goals happen for you at the time you wanted them to? Probably not as many as you would like. It happens to the majority of people, and that's why not everyone is successful.

Goal setting for success

Goal setting is hard and can be extremely emotional. When you don't achieve the goals that you've set, you become disappointed. Over time, it gets harder and harder for you to set goals for your future if you have failed in the past.

Emotions from past failures rise up into your present and affect how you set goals for your future. This limits you and prevents you from reaching your full potential.

When you set your goals effectively and take the right action steps, you achieve your goals and create your new reality, both physically and emotionally. It's time to be awesome at goal setting.

Don't skip this chapter or dismiss the importance of goal setting. You may think you're good at goal setting already or have convinced yourself that the *doing* is more important than the *planning* and the *time management* of getting the things done. The opposite is actually true.

Once you are in the *busy mode of doing*, you lose sight of the big picture. A few months can go by before you realize you have yet to reach your goal. What's worse is that you look ahead and see there isn't enough time left to achieve your goal, and you become defeated. Why? You extrapolate the success (or lack of it) that you have had in the past, out into the future, as your only possible future outcome. This is a dangerous way to set goals because it sets you up for failure.

In this chapter, I will teach you how to set goals effectively and take the right actions to achieve them to create your new reality.

Set goals effectively to create your new reality

"Setting goals is the first step in turning the invisible into the visible." – Tony Robbins

Your goals must be challenging but based in reality so that:
- you can commit to your goals
- you can believe you can accomplish them
- you have the goals working for you instead of you working for your goals

The best way to help you understand this is to use my own story of my first year on Zazzle.

Case Study

When I first started on Zazzle, my goal was to replace my career salary ($100,000) with my Zazzle earnings in my first year. It was a huge goal, and I did not *add a touch of reality* to my goal setting.

Unfortunately, I only made $90. Why did I fail to achieve my goal? It's obviously possible because, for the past 7 years, I have earned over $100K yearly on Zazzle, by selling over 1 million dollars' worth of products every year.

Why did it not happen in my first year? It is because I did not set the right realistic action steps to reach my high financial goal.

After working hard in my first year, and only making $90 in income, I was absolutely mortified, and I was convinced I had made the biggest mistake of my life. I doubted my every choice I made on my Zazzle store, and I was incapable of getting much work done. I loved staying home with my kids, and I knew in my heart that this is where I needed to be. But all my decisions about what to do with Zazzle were made with fear and uncertainty. I used my poor results to define my future potential, and I allowed it to influence both my attitude and goal setting.

Had I set my action steps properly a year earlier, I would not have wasted more time in my emotionally distressed state before I could create results and move forward.

I should have kept revising either my goal or my actions during the year, using the outcomes I saw, on a monthly basis.

Instead, what I did was hope things would improve, while working harder, doing the same things over and over again, without understanding the reality of how I could achieve my goal.

TAKE ACTION:
Be realistic in setting your action steps to achieve your goal. A bigger goal just requires bigger action steps. *Read this next section, and then write your ultimate earnings goal for the next year, in the "Notes" section at the end of this chapter.*

Then, use your ultimate earnings goal to figure out what you need to sell monthly to achieve this goal. Write your sales per month goal down in the "Notes," along with which scenario (similar to one of the scenarios listed below) will make you achieve your goal. Write your scenario down.

Finally, decide what your absolute first "next step" is to achieve this goal, and write this down in the "Notes" as well. Do not worry that there are multiple steps involved. You can only take one step at a time. Once it is complete, you can know what the next step is and take it.

Consider the following before completing the action steps noted above. Being realistic does not mean aiming low. Instead, it means that if you are going to set your goal high, then you also need to take the right action steps that will realistically make you achieve your goal. That could mean working more productive hours, making more products, or using proven methods to speed up how soon you will begin earning money, and how fast the sales multiply.

How to come up with realistic scenarios to achieve your big goal

"Goals are pure fantasy unless you have a specific plan to achieve them."
– Stephen Covey

I could have earned 100K in my first year, but to do that, I would have had to use an entirely different approach in my goal setting than what I did. Had I found ways to realistically make this type of money, and implement them, I would not have struggled so hard.

I was posting products for sale that would pay me, on average, $1 royalty per sale per customer. I was not being realistic. In my mind, I *hoped* it was possible to sell to 100,000 customers by doing nothing but putting up my products for sale. I did not market the products; I did not strategically create the right products, with different royalty payouts; and more.

I did not understand that in order to achieve my goal, I had to create the situation in which I would physically make my goal possible. To do that, I should have been aware of what it would take, and put things in place to make it happen. But first, I had to look at the realistic scenarios and figure out which ones I could accomplish.

Here are some examples of realistic scenarios:

- If I had created a massive marketing campaign to sell my one product (at $1 royalty) to 1 million people, with a 1% success rate (i.e. 100K buy, which is industry standard), then I would have achieved my earnings goal of 100K.
- If I had created a massive marketing campaign to sell 2 products (each at $5 royalty) to 100K people, with a 1% success rate (i.e. 10K buy, which is industry standard), then I would have achieved my earnings goal of 100K.
- If I had created 100 products (at $1 royalty), and each sold once, to 1,000 people, then I would have achieved my earnings goal of 100K.
- If I had created 200 products (at $5 royalty), and each sold once, to 100 people, then I would have achieved my earnings goal of 100K.
- If I had created 100 products (at $10 royalty), and each sold once, to 100 people, then I would have achieved my earnings goal of 100K.
- If I had created 100 products (at $5 royalty), and each sold once, to 200 people, then I would have achieved my earnings goal of 100K.

By creating these realistic scenarios, your method of achieving a goal goes from one of *hope* to one of calculated planning and implementation of steps to achieve the goal. Your mind is also able to *see* these outcomes as more possible than just aiming for the elusive *$100K* as a large number.

Let's take example #6. It has been broken down into a manageable goal now, to achieve what seemed like an unmanageable result in your mind ($100K).

Your action steps can now be defined more clearly:
- Make products or groups of products that generate, on average, $5 royalty or higher per sale.
- Post 1,000 products for sale (based on a success rate of 1 sale out of every 10 products).
- Promote 100 products that ultimately sell to 200 people, at a $5 royalty.

This example walks you through the process so that you can now do this to set your goals and then define your action steps accordingly. Once you go through this exercise, you can see the scope more clearly. Also, at that point, you can decide if you are up for the challenge or if you have to scale down your goal for that year, to align with what you feel is a challenging but manageable action step.

"The path to success is to take massive, determined action." – Tony Robbins

TAKE ACTION:
Review the instructions in the last *YOUR ACTION STEPS* section, and then, in the "Notes" section at the end of this chapter, write the items requested, using all the information provided here in this section.

You must have successful habit goals to make a big change

"Successful people are simply those with successful habits." – Brian Tracey

Setting a financial goal and action steps does not ensure success. You must also change your current habits of productivity. You must set successful habit goals.

To help you understand what this means, note whether you answer "Yes" or "No" to the following questions:

- Do you get things done when you schedule them?
- Do you get distracted easily?
- Do you find that hours slip by, and you have not accomplished what you want, even though you have been working hard?
- Do you put things off because you don't want to do them?
- Do you never get to something important because *life* gets in the way?

If you answered yes to one or more of these questions, then you have just proven to yourself that you have bad productivity habits, and you need new constructive habit goals. It does not mean you are a poor worker, or that you are a bad person. It just means that you are like most people in the world. You don't have the right habits and tools to change those habits into more productive ones that create a more productive you.

Changing habits is not easy, but once you consistently choose a productive habit goal, you will begin to form a new habit for yourself, which will be long lasting.

"For changes to be of any true value, they've got to be lasting and consistent."
– Tony Robbins

What are some ways you can get started quickly to change your working habits? The best way to start is slow and steady, with one change at a time. Also, you must keep in mind that habits are not changed overnight. It takes about 30 days of consistent, daily implementation of the new habit for it to become your regular habit.

Set a productivity habit goal

You can tackle productivity by choosing to practice a technique that increases productivity, like the Pomodoro Technique. It is a time management method developed by Francesco Cirillo, in the late 1980s. The technique uses a timer to break down work into intervals, traditionally 25 minutes in length, separated by short breaks. The intervals, called *pomodoros* (Italian for tomato), are called that because of the tomato-shaped kitchen timer he used.

It's a simple technique to help you to keep track of time and create a connection between a time interval and your productivity. Typically, 20 to 25 minutes is the length of time people can focus efficiently on a task before they lose interest or become less productive. It's a good idea to get up, move around, and take a 5-minute break before starting another interval of efficient work.

TAKE ACTION:

Try the Pomodoro Technique for about an hour's work time, and write your observations in the "Notes" at the end of this chapter. Did it work for you? Break the hour into 25-minute intervals and see how it goes. Were you more productive compared to working for an hour straight without a break?

Are you going to use this technique daily for the next 30 days to make it a permanent habit? If so, mark it in your calendar and review your progress in 30 days. If it does not work, research other productivity techniques, and try one for 30 days.

Set an overcoming distraction habit goal

Tackling distractions is tough, but you can do it. First, note what your distractions are. Then make plans to avoid them, even for 1 hour, in order to create a habit of clearing distractions quickly, just before you start working on an important task.

Below are questions that prompt you to think of examples of distractions. Then I provide you with solutions to create habit goals to solve them.

- Is it your physical surroundings in your house, with kids, or other obligations? Then you need to create a peaceful work environment, and block time in your calendar for just you.

- Is it your social media, emails, or YouTube notifications? Turn them off (or deal with them first) for a designated time so that you can then work without distractions.

- Is it procrastination, and allowing yourself to be distracted to avoid getting things done? Find out why you are procrastinating, and solve that problem. Could it be that you are not in the right mindset?

TAKE ACTION:
In the "Notes" section at the end of this chapter, write the top 3 ways you get distracted from completing your tasks. Then take each one and write a habit goal to create a solution, like the ones suggested above.

Failure equals opportunity

"Failure is simply the opportunity to begin again, this time more intelligently."
– Henry Ford

Always consider a failure as an opportunity to learn and improve. Failures are gifts of discovery, to confirm that something did not work in a certain way. Failures are results in the big experiment of building a business. The sooner you can identify your failures, the sooner you can grow beyond them.

Failures can give you the opportunity to do several important things to grow your business and be successful. First, they confirm that a particular way does not work. Second, they force you to find a new approach, which may be the one that finally works. Third, anticipating failure allows you to plan for it by having measures in place to assess if a failure is occurring, and to act on it fast. Finally, actions to avoid or minimize failures can also be put in place, such as following a proven plan, and receiving guidance from successful people right from the start.

Failure, both personal and business, cannot be an excuse to give up or not allow your business to grow to your dream goal. Your decision to use instances of failure as a way to learn and grow sets you apart from many other entrepreneurs, and gives you more chance of succeeding.

The best way to use failure to your advantage is to have a process already worked out as to how to recognize when it has happened, and how you will deal with the failure on a personal and emotional level, as well as within your business.

TAKE ACTION:
In the "Notes" section at the end of this chapter, create your action plan for handling failure. How will you recognize when failure has happened, and how will you deal with the failure on a personal and emotional level, as well as within your business?

Take ownership of the good and the bad

"Success consists of going from failure to failure, without loss of enthusiasm."
– Winston Churchill

Remember that you are responsible for this business. You are NOT a pawn in the game of life. You need to take ownership and be responsible for both your successes and failures, and your attitude towards each of them.

This is extremely important advice. Taking ownership is a key component for the success of your business. If you care for it, you will make the right decisions.

If you face your failures and the bad times head on, and see them as opportunities, then you will achieve success. No successful company around today grew without their share of bad times. If you know to expect this, and take ownership of it when it happens, then you retain the power to do something about it.

How to solve each situation will be different, but in each case, you must first recognize it and take ownership of the issue. Once you do that, you will confidently find ways to grow, and solve whatever is causing the *bad* to happen.

"The greatest glory in living lies not in never falling, but in rising every time we fall." – Ralph Waldo Emerson

Make sure you also take time out of your day to celebrate the good, and truly allow yourself to experience the joy of accomplishment. These moments of achievement must be valued, announced, celebrated, and acknowledged.

Here are a few suggestions on how you can celebrate:
- You can choose the event beforehand and have it set as a reward if a specific task is completed, or a certain result is achieved.
- You can be spontaneous and choose a celebratory option based on the current situation.
- Choose a way to celebrate that is in line with the event or result (i.e. small achievement, small event, etc.)
- Celebrate both the small and the big accomplishments.

TAKE ACTION:
In the "Notes" section at the end of this chapter, write one way in which you will celebrate small accomplishments, like daily achievements, and then one way you will celebrate if you reach a huge goal or result. A small celebration can be a dinner out. A big celebration can be a vacation.

Put your results in perspective

"I have not failed. I've just found 10,000 ways that won't work."
– Thomas Edison

Thank goodness, Thomas Edison did not give up. If he would have given up because he had the wrong perspective about his results, then we would all still be using candlelight.

Would you have given up earlier than 10,000 tries? Having 10,000 failures behind him, his optimism must have increased, because he was soon going to come up with the working prototype. Ask yourself honestly if you could have that type of perspective. It definitely worked for Thomas Edison.

When monitoring your results and comparing them to your goals, it is important to look at them with perspective as well. You can also use this perspective as a motivator.

For example, let's say your goal is to earn 100K in one year on Zazzle. By the end of the year, you earned $95K. Would you consider this a failure because you did not earn 100K? If you said yes, then you have the wrong perspective. Would you rather beat yourself up because you didn't earn that last 5K, or would you be overjoyed because you were only 5K away from reaching your goal? You earned $95K! That is a fantastic achievement and is as good as earning $100K.

At the end of the year, celebrate your actual achievement rather than focusing on the gap between your goal and your actual outcome.

Let's keep going with this example. At the beginning of the year, you have earned 5K, and want to reach 100K. You can be discouraged because the gap seems so big. Instead, be inspired that you have already made 5K. You can also be challenged and motivated to close the gap between the actual earnings and the earnings goal.

At the beginning of the year, use this gap as a motivator to push harder to achieve your goal, as well as celebrating the smaller amount you have already earned.

TAKE ACTION:
In the "Notes" section, write down one example of when you were discouraged about a result, even though you had achieved 80 to 90% of your goal. Then write down how differently you would have made subsequent decisions if you had put the result in perspective and had celebrated it rather than engulfing it in negative thoughts.

Use the right plan of action

"If you do what you've always done, you'll get what you've always gotten."
– Tony Robbins

The reality of the situation is that whatever you are currently doing to achieve your goal, it is giving you your current result. If you are not earning the money you want, then that means your current plan of action is not the one you should be continuing to follow.

Have you ever tried to lose weight, and failed over and over again with each new diet? Then, one day, you try another diet, thinking that it will fail too, but it works! What happened?

You used a plan of action that was designed for weight loss, just like all the other diets. But this one suited how your body type metabolizes food. You finally used the plan of action (diet, in this example) that worked specifically for you.

To achieve your Zazzle earnings goal, you must find the right plan of action that will work specifically for you. You must initially use a plan that is a proven plan, and one that tailors to how you work. Then, as you define and grow your business, you will add your specifics to this core proven plan, so that it continually works for you.

That is what makes The 5 Step Profit Plan™ so powerful. On the one hand, it provides the exact steps to become successful, but it allows you to customize it to suit your needs, how you work, and what your unique skills are.

Case Study

Hundreds of people are members in The 5 Step Profit Plan VIP Mentoring Program™, yet not everyone is equally successful. Why is that?

The 5 Step Profit Plan™ works. But different mindsets, work habits, personal drives to succeed, earnings goals, and various life situations are just some of the reasons responsible for why not everyone has the same outcome using the same plan.

It's actually quite common in all walks of life. Recall when you were in high school. Same teacher, same subject, same text book, same lessons—yet not everyone got the same grade. It's because we are not all the same, and we need to develop the parts of ourselves that are also necessary components to be successful at ANYTHING in life, not just building our Zazzle business.

That is why I am spending so much time in this book on other aspects besides the physical steps to creating a Zazzle business. In fact, STEP 1 in The 5 Step Profit Plan™ is all about working on yourself. You have to have clear goals, be in the right mindset, have good work habits, avoid being dictated to by fear and procrastination, and above all, take full ownership for the success of your business.

A great example is Brandon. I have talked about him because he sold over $100K worth of Zazzle products, one year after starting The 5 Step Profit Plan VIP Mentoring Program™. At the one-year mark, when Brandon was reviewing how his year went, he realized that he was the reason why his success was actually less than it already was.

He had taken some time off, just as his Zazzle business was taking off—not a good business decision. He had created a story for himself about why he didn't need to ask me for more mentoring help. Once I nudged him to take action and use my advice, he saw huge increases in sales. Brandon, at that point, regretted not asking me for help sooner. It was only after he had gone through this experience that he became aware of what he had lost, by not taking action and not being aware of his own destructive habits and decisions.

That is why the mentoring program works so well alongside The 5 Step Profit Plan™. A mentor has been through the journey already and is further along than where you want to be. A mentor can also see things that are staring you right in the face, when you can't. A mentor is there to help you face facts and force you (in a gentle way) to make the hard decisions.

Elke's Secret to Success

A plan that has been proven to achieve your goal, and a mentor that has already achieved what you want to achieve, are the keys to success.

Summary

In this chapter, I taught you how to set goals effectively, and take the right actions to achieve them in order to create your new reality. In the next chapter, I will show you techniques that will help you achieve these goals.

Notes:

Chapter 7:

Think and Act Like a Successful Entrepreneur

"Our goals can only be reached through a vehicle of a plan, in which we must fervently believe, and upon which we must vigorously act. There is no other route to success."
– Pablo Picasso

In the previous chapter, you learned how to set goals and what to do to achieve them. In this chapter, you will learn about why thinking and acting like a successful entrepreneur is a key factor in achieving your goals.

Believing you can become a successful entrepreneur, and acting like one, even before you achieve your goal, is a powerful method that I use to achieve success. I recommend you use it as well. This does not mean that you spend like a millionaire and lead a lavish lifestyle. Instead, it is a mind game you play with yourself.

When I first began reading self-help books, I was not ready mentally to believe that my mind could be so powerful. I doubted that I could *trick* myself into believing, even though I wanted to believe the logic, advice, and messages.

But as I continued to read books, like *Think and Grow Rich,* by Napoleon Hill; *The Power of Positive Thinking,* by Norman Vincent Peale; *The Science of Getting Rich,* by Wallace D. Wattles; *Secrets of the Millionaire Mind,* by T. Harv Eker; *Awaken the Giant Within,* by Tony Robbins; and *The Secret,* by Rhonda Byrne, I put more and more of their teachings into practice. I began to see results. The reinforcement of achieving results created new habits in me that are responsible for my continued success. These are the habits of thinking and acting as if I had already achieved my goals.

The biggest changes happened when I began to think and act like I was already successful at what I set out to achieve.

Believe that you are a successful entrepreneur

"I believe any success in life is made by going into an area with a blind, furious optimism." – Sylvester Stallone

The power of positive thinking has been proven time and time again. When you believe you can achieve your goal, you will achieve it. You are sending messages to your subconscious mind when you consciously tell yourself that you can achieve your goal, or that you are grateful that you have already achieved it.

Your subconscious mind starts to work on how you can achieve that goal. You begin to think of opportunities and possibilities, because your mind is open to achieving your goal. Consciously, you may not know how to get there; but subconsciously, your brain is looking for opportunities to make your goal a reality.

Very few successful entrepreneurs, when they first started out, actually knew how they would achieve their goal. They just knew, with clarity and unwavering certainty, that they would be successful.

Whatever you tell yourself is possible will become a reality.

Your brain does not know the difference between right and wrong, or between a small or large income goal. It only knows what you provide it as information. If you say 100K is a large amount of money and hard to earn, then that will be the truth in your reality. But it is not hard for some people to earn 100K, or even greater amounts of money, and they have the same abilities as you do. What's the difference?

Successful people do not think limiting thoughts. They believe anything is possible.

This mindset of one number being harder to achieve than another is all based on your past experience, and only exists in your head. It is your LEARNED response to past outcomes of past experiences. That means you can also UNLEARN this response and replace it with a new belief.

If you believe you can make 100K, then you can also believe you can make 1 million. Why not increase your goal and aim for the higher number? The only thing standing in your way is your own belief that you have set for yourself. You can undo your limiting belief.

Act like a successful entrepreneur

"Success or failure depends more upon attitude than upon capacity. Successful men act as though they have accomplished or are enjoying something. Soon it becomes a reality. Act, look, feel successful, conduct yourself accordingly, and you will be amazed at the positive results." – William James

Most people, right away, think that when they are told to *act like a successful person*, they should go out and spend money. That is not what "act like a successful entrepreneur" means.

What "act like a successful entrepreneur" really means is to make choices like a successful entrepreneur in your business. Plan for the future. Take calculated risks. See the potential of a business opportunity. Plan to succeed. Learn from mistakes and failures. Keep striving ahead, and don't let issues stop you from achieving your ultimate goal. Most importantly, act as if you expect success to happen.

A successful entrepreneur expects success to happen.

TAKE ACTION:
Write down in the "Notes" at the end of this chapter, your answers to the following questions, with brutal honesty.

- Do you believe you can succeed at whatever you desire?

- Do you set your goals, without hindrance from your own limiting beliefs?
- What limiting beliefs do you need to overcome to allow you to move forward with your dream goals?
- What do you think you would accomplish with your current limiting beliefs?
- What do you think you can accomplish if you believed and acted like a successful entrepreneur?

Banish the F-Word

"If you want to conquer fear, don't sit at home and think about it. Go out and get busy." – Dale Carnegie

This quote, by Dale Carnegie, is a great approach to take when faced with any one of your fears. Instead of letting your fear paralyze you to the point of inaction, just do it. It's easy to understand this advice, but a lot harder to actually act on it.

When my mentoring program members ask me for help because they are *stuck,* most of the time, the reason is because they are afraid of something: afraid of failure, afraid of what their family and friends will say, afraid of not being good enough to sell well on Zazzle, afraid of not making enough money to be able to quit their day job, afraid of accomplishing their goal, afraid of being successful. That's right, it's sometimes even the fear of success, even though they are 100% committed to succeeding to achieve their goal.

Fear is a menacing beast that must be banished from your life in order to succeed.

Most fears stem from a fear of failure.

Banish the fear of failure, and success will seek you out.

Fear of failure is an incredibly strong motivator for you to act contrary to your best interests. Fear of failure can rule your mind and your actions, to the point where you are convinced that your actions of avoidance make sense and are the best for you.

Have you ever caught yourself procrastinating, even though the thing that needs to get done could make a huge difference in your life and stop you from struggling?

Case Study

I can recount many times in my life when I made a decision out of fear of failure, rather than in my best interest for achieving my best successful future. I know I would have had greater success than I currently have if I had not acted out of fear in certain situations in the past. It is only in hindsight that I recognize how my decisions affected me negatively and held me back.

My advice is to learn from my mistakes.

When I was making the decision, I honestly thought I was doing the right thing. I was so wrong. I am going to tell you a story about what happened to me in one case where my fear was so great. It caused me to act out of fear, and yet the action to overcome the fear was so minor. After this happened to me, I realized how much I was letting my life be run by fear. I was missing out on the success I wanted so badly. It was a turning point in my life.

When I first started on Zazzle, I had no graphic design experience. I added my artwork and photography to Zazzle products, but I noticed that graphic designs were selling well. I knew I had to take advantage of this opportunity to increase my earnings on Zazzle, but I was fearful of so many things, and that stopped me from getting started.

I feared learning a new program (Adobe Photoshop) so that I could create the graphics. I feared that I would not recoup the cost of buying the license for the program. I feared that my designs would not be as good as what was selling on Zazzle. I feared the competition on Zazzle, and I convinced myself that I was wasting my time learning what I needed to learn. I feared that I would not stay true to my art and photography career that I thought I was building for myself. I even feared the act of starting because it was something new and would take me out of my comfort zone.

It sounds crazy, but for me, at the time, it felt absolutely true, and it dictated my actions.

What I did not realize, at the time, was that these fears had me convinced that I didn't need to learn the graphic design program. I convinced myself that I could work around it by making designs on the Zazzle design tool. This backfired because I took way too long to make things. It wasted time I could have used to work productively. I was limited in what I could accomplish using this approach, and thus did not have the best product designs available for sale.

This resulted in lost sales opportunities. Also, the way I was compensating for not using the graphics files created a problem in the future when Zazzle changed something in their design tool. From one moment to the next, thousands of my designs were completely *messed up*, and no longer desirable for purchase: design elements were missing; they were the wrong size; or they were shifted in position. My designs on my products went from looking good to completely unsellable. The time I had taken to make these designs was wasted, and I had to start again.

I had wasted so much time out of fear; time in which I could have already been selling products. If I had not been fearful of learning the graphics program, I would have created the right kind of designs, sooner and more professionally, without issues of my designs being completely useless from one moment to the next.

I also would have sold more products earlier on and had time to continue to make more desirable designs and products sooner. I paid dearly for not banishing the F-Word (fear) and learning the graphics design program, when I first realized that I needed to take advantage of this opportunity.

My fear was so great that it took me about 2 years to finally sit down for a few hours and learn how to use Adobe Photoshop. It sounds ridiculous now, but it was such an overwhelming fear for me that I would procrastinate and give myself reasons for not doing it, and even experienced physical symptoms whenever I even thought of getting started.

Once I had finally spent those few hours and tackled my fear, I instantly realized how much I had let fear control my ability to achieve success.

I am now vigilant when such a strong fear comes over me. I explain to myself that it will be uncomfortable, I will have doubts, I will find ways to avoid doing it, but it is obviously what I have to do. The stronger the feeling of fear for things that are not physically harmful to you, the more significant they are to overcome. Overcoming these fears will move you the furthest forward on your journey to success.

Take risks with attitude

"The trouble is, if you don't risk anything, you risk even more."
– Erica Jong

Today, I make much better decisions, and I realize that my fears were unfounded and self-imposed. Instead, I use the energy my fears create, to catapult me to where I need to go.

When you are terrified of failure, you instinctively don't take the risk. However, if you do risk taking that first step, you will realize that failure is only part of your journey and not the end result. Failure is not absolute or final.

Each failure moves you closer to the best version of *you* that you can be in this life.

If you look at successful people that you admire, you will be amazed at how many failures each of them has overcome on their journey to success.

If you view failure as an opportunity and a necessary step to success, then you banish fear.

When you replace your fear with the knowledge that you will emerge stronger and wiser from experiencing failures, you will be secure in your ability to take on, survive, and thrive in any situation.

When you banish fear, you will take the risks. When you take risks, you will be on your way to achieving the level of success you were meant to achieve.

TAKE ACTION:
In the "Notes" at the end of this chapter, list 3 failures you have experienced in your business and in your life, and what they have taught you. Also, write down what you accomplished after you failed in these instances. Would you have achieved these accomplishments had you not first had these failures?

Be quick to recover and rise up

"Our greatest glory is not in never failing, but in rising up every time we fail."
– Ralph Waldo Emerson

You will experience big and small failures in your journey through life. Give yourself some time to recover, and to heal and nurture your soul; but put a time limit on your recovery, and set an expectation to not bring the negativity of the failure into your future. This seems harsh and almost impossible, but it is the key to moving forward and not giving up.

Your goal is to ensure that you acknowledge the failure you just experienced, but you do not need to be affected by it moving forward, except to learn that you are strong and can survive failure.

If you do some honest soul searching, you will find many examples in your life where you gave up on your big dream, or maybe even on small goals, because you are still *recovering* from your past failures. In your mind, you have allowed past failures to shape your opinion of what you can accomplish in the future. This is why you are being held back from achieving what you want.

You use your past failures as a way to justify and validate statements that you make to yourself: I always fail; it's not meant to be; the universe is not on my side; I never succeed; why try, I'm just going to fail again anyway.

If these thoughts are going through your mind, you are in the unhealthy victim mode. You are justifying why you can't move out of the past and into the present. You need to stop these thoughts immediately, and counterstrike by taking action to move toward your goal.

"Many of life's failures are people who did not realize how close they were to success when they gave up." – Thomas Edison

When you were little and learning to walk, did you stay on the ground after falling down the first time you tried to stand up? Did you have a conversation with yourself about how you were obviously not meant to walk, and that you should just crawl for the rest of your life? Of course not! Life has not changed. You are still facing obstacles and experiencing failures. It is only your thoughts about failures, and how you consciously choose to react to those failures, that has changed.

The good news for you is that since these are just thoughts, they can be changed. You can choose to change how you think about failure and how you react to it.

Choose to recover fast and never give up.

TAKE ACTION:
In the "Notes" section at the end of this chapter, write an affirmation that you can say to yourself each time you begin to slide into a pity party about your circumstances. Here is an example:

"With every failure, big or small, I choose to overcome my emotions of pity and doubt, to recover quickly emotionally, stay in the present, never give up, and move forward with the knowledge that I have the strength to survive and the ability to succeed."

Surround yourself with positivity

Have you ever been down or stressed, and then you meet someone who is positive and in a good mood? What happened to you? Your mood improved, right? Have you had the opposite occur, where you are feeling good, and a negative person you meet brings you down with their words and body language? What is even worse is that you might currently be surrounded by these negative people all day long, because they are your wife, husband, children, relatives, friends, boss, or coworkers.

If you are creative, you are most likely more acutely aware and dramatically affected by your surroundings. This includes day to day environments and the beliefs of others with whom you interact. Have you ever felt upbeat and full of energy on a sunny spring day? On a dreary, grey winter's day, have you looked outside and wanted to stay under the covers in bed all day?

Do you modify your responses and choices based on the people around you? Would you feel deflated if someone told you that "online money-making opportunities are not a *real* job?" They are telling you this because they don't understand, never want to, and are more interested in deflecting attention from the situation. In the meantime, their words have negatively impacted you.

A person's words and actions, positive or negative, impact you because your brain has no filter—except in the situation where you consciously say, "No! This will not affect me!" Your brain takes on the environment you surround yourself with, positive or negative.

In order to succeed and change your life to the one you dream of living, you must surround yourself with positive, encouraging people. If you can't find those in your current environment, make it a high priority to surround yourself with people who will lift up your spirits, help you banish your fears, and support you in achieving your goals.

Case Study

When I first started on Zazzle, in 2007, my family and friends did not trust that making money online was a viable business opportunity. They thought I was wasting my time on Zazzle, and kept telling me to "get a real job." I was told I had wasted my university education by pursuing what I really loved and wanted to do.

They constantly asked how much I was making, with the purpose of reminding me that I was not making much money in those first few years. It was extremely difficult to push on and believe that I could make my dream come true.

I began to look for other like-minded people who were positive and encouraging, while doing my best to drown out the negative influences around me.

Fast forward to today, and those naysayers are now asking me how they can be successful like I am. At the time of writing this book, I had sold over 10 million dollars' worth of Zazzle products. Sales have continually been in the 7-figures, every year.

Due to my success on Zazzle, and the requests of so many people like yourself to tell them how I did it, I have created The 5 Step Profit Plan Program™. To join, visit https://elkeclarke.com/profit/, and find out how you can be part of a positive community of like-minded Zazzle designers, who are reaching their Zazzle earnings goals using The 5 Step Profit Plan Program™.

Have an attitude of gratitude mindset

"As we express our gratitude, we must never forget that the highest appreciation is not to utter words but to live by them."
– John F. Kennedy

I will be honest with you. The road to becoming a creative online millionaire like me will not be smooth, and you will not take a direct route, but it will be easier and quicker with The 5 Step Profit Plan Program™.

Also, many people have already achieved what you want to achieve on Zazzle, so you know it is possible. These people have achieved their Zazzle success recently, so you cannot use the excuse that it is too late to be successful.

The secret to success is to follow and implement a proven plan, and to use a mentor who is successful on Zazzle, to guide you and maintain an attitude of gratitude.

If you can be grateful for even the smallest of things, then you will be overjoyed at the big accomplishments. More importantly, you will take the bumps in the road with more positive gratitude than negative attitude. This will help you get over negative issues sooner, and minimize your wasted time getting back on track. It will also help you see opportunities where others would see roadblocks.

TAKE ACTION:
In the "Notes" section at the end of this chapter, write the statement...

"I always have an attitude of gratitude."

Then put action steps into place to ensure that this is your daily attitude. Create reminders for yourself—like a screensaver with the statement on it—and write it out in your journal; or you can purchase motivational products with this statement on them, at https://www.zazzle.com/creativemillionaire.

I have designed these products on Zazzle so that you can benefit from this powerful technique, like I did while I was growing my business. I always use this technique, even now that I am successful. It works so well for me, and it will for you too, if you do it correctly.

Elke's Secret to Success

Attitude is everything—a cliché but true. You attract your circumstances. Choose to attract wealth and positivity.

Summary

In this chapter, you learned about the importance of thinking and acting like a successful entrepreneur in order to achieve your earnings goals and grow your online business through Zazzle.

I told you about my story of how I lost many opportunities because I let fear hold me back. You also learned about the importance of taking risks and being grateful for failures. If you don't fail, you won't learn from your mistakes and grow to become the successful entrepreneur you can be.

Surrounding yourself with positive influencers and having an attitude of gratitude are vital to your ability to be resilient to negative situations, which could have the potential to stop you from achieving your dream goals.

In the next chapter, I teach you about money; how to unblock your money barriers; how to use your money wisely, personally and in business; how to leverage plus and minus points about Zazzle; and how your Zazzle business is an investment that can generate money for you for years to come.

Notes:

Chapter 8:

What About the Money?

"All money is a matter of belief." – Adam Smith

Unblock your own money mindset barriers

I have told you about my journey to Zazzle success. You have read about the story of Brandon, who used The 5 Step Profit Plan VIP Mentoring Program™ to achieve success on Zazzle. There are many other successful Zazzle designers who have earned 6 and 7-figure incomes from Zazzle. Zazzle has paid out 100+ million dollars to Zazzle designers in the form of royalties. (https://www.zazzle.com/10th.)

In this book, I have told you what you can do to accomplish your Zazzle earnings goal, and I have provided you with many tools and resources to ensure that you will be successful; yet you may still not be able to make your dream a reality because you are missing one essential component.

The essential component to your monetary success is your money mindset.

Your money beliefs play a big role in whether or not you will achieve your monetary goal. You inherited your money mindset—your beliefs about money and how it can be earned—from your parents, relatives, and friends, at an early age, and they have stayed with you into adulthood. You may not even be aware of them, or think there is a problem, because everyone around you has similar money beliefs.

It's only when you attempt to make a big change in your monetary status, like making money in a different way and in larger amounts than you are used to, that you become aware of your money mindset barriers and how they are holding you back from achieving your goal.

Let's address some of the common money mindset barriers.

Money mindset barrier – Mistrust of the income source

The first barrier that can stop you from making money online with Zazzle is the mistrust of Zazzle itself as a legitimate income source. This mistrust might have originated from what you have learned from online reviews, and by word of mouth, about ways to make money online in general. There are definitely online money-making schemes out there that you should be cautious about, but Zazzle is legitimate.

There are also reviews online and in the Zazzle forums, by Zazzle designers who have complained that they are not selling on Zazzle. As well, there are other posts from people who feel cheated by Zazzle for changes that have taken place, which have affected them in a negative way. These stories are easy to relate to and believe, and they could also be your explanation for why you are not succeeding. I caution you to not get sucked in to the negative drama of excuses. Look at the bigger picture instead of taking the easy way out of the situation and accepting someone else's excuse to not succeed.

It is up to you to decide if you feel that the negative comments are truly warranted, or if there is more going on with the people making these negative statements.

Case Study

During my Zazzle mentoring and coaching, I have come across many people who have this initial negative perception of Zazzle. After I work with them and dig deeper, I find the mistrust is a way they have chosen to use to deal with their own situation. In actual fact, they did not have the right tools and guidance to make money on Zazzle. As soon as they implement the 5 steps, which I teach in The 5 Step Profit Plan™, they see results. They also gain perspective and come to realize that their money mindset was a barrier that resulted in their negative experience that they had with Zazzle in the past. They had interpreted the situation happening to them with limited ability to see other options for themselves. In the end, it was not a mistrust in the income source, but a fear of the unknown, and the lack of a proven strategy and tools to succeed.

Zazzle is a legitimate online income opportunity that has been a reliable and consistent income source for me and hundreds of thousands of others for many years. In 2015, Zazzle celebrated it's 10th anniversary. You can check out the special website that Zazzle made in honor of their 10-year anniversary, at the links provided. You will see that I am featured on this Zazzle website page as the top seller: https://www.zazzle.com/10th. I am not an employee of Zazzle, and I am not endorsed by Zazzle. My recognition on this 10th anniversary page was purely because I had achieved financial success on my own, using Zazzle to sell my graphic designs, photography, and art.

At that time, in 2015, Zazzle reported that there were over 600K Zazzle designers who had opened Zazzle stores, and that Zazzle had paid out more than 100 million dollars US, to date, to Zazzle designers.

Since Zazzle is a private company, the information on the website was the last time Zazzle publicly reported this type of data. I can only imagine it has continued to grow. I have also continued to make substantial earnings on Zazzle since 2015, reaching the million-dollar mark in 2017.

Money mindset barrier – Ethical

Has someone you know told you that there are ethical and not so ethical ways to make money? Have you ever heard the phrase, *"You have to work hard to make money?"* Has online income, or passive income, fallen under the not-so-ethical side? *"There must be a catch; it must be a scam."* If you have heard any of these statements, you are not alone. I still get these types of comments now, despite having proven that I consistently earn 6 figures, year after year, online, using Zazzle.

Consider from whom these statements come from. Is that person someone who has traditional views on how money can be made? Does that person think you should *"get a real job?"* Has that person been at the same company for their entire life, and is scared of any type of entrepreneurial way to make money? If a person is ingrained with the mindset that the only way to make money is in a traditional salaried job, then that person will have a hard time accepting it, and would rather put it down.

Your relatives, friends, and coworkers may never truly understand that making money online with Zazzle is a reality for the 600K+ Zazzle designers around the world. It's not their fault. The concept is becoming more mainstream, but many people have not yet had enough positive experience with making money online to accept it as a viable option. But as I pointed out, those who have accepted it and embraced it, like me, have benefited greatly.

That is why I am sharing my story, and those of others, with you here in this book. It is possible to make a substantial income from Zazzle. The people who you love and trust may still not believe it is possible, or trust that Zazzle is a viable option to make money and earn a living consistently, year after year. You might just have to accept it, as I have done.

Family and friends thought I was wasting my time, and they kept telling me I should *"get my old 9 to 5 job back."* Their comments could have stopped me, but I believed that it was possible to make money with Zazzle, and I made it happen. Had I listened to the advice of people who were stuck in this limiting money mindset, with a mistrust for non-traditional ways to make money, I would not be a millionaire right now.

Obviously, now my relatives, friends, and former coworkers are extremely interested in how I achieved my online success on Zazzle. What you have to understand, though, is that most of them still don't really *get it.* They are happy for me, but they would never feel comfortable taking that *risk* themselves, because they mistrust nontraditional ways to make money. They don't have the experience to feel comfortable to change their mindset or beliefs about making money online. Due to this mindset, they will still warn you and advise you against it, using many different tactics.

It is up to you to decide what perspective a person has, and why they are making the comments they are making, in order to interpret their advice properly.

Money mindset barrier – Lack of abundance

When you first start on Zazzle, you might search online to find out what the top sellers on Zazzle make. Or you might search phrases, such as, "Can you really make money on Zazzle?" "How much can you make on Zazzle?" Can you become a millionaire with Zazzle?"

I actually searched these phrases myself when I first started. I had all of these money mindset barriers I have told you about, and I needed to overcome them before I could achieve success. I had a *mistrust of the income source.* I wondered if I could *ethically make money online.* But the biggest hurdle, for me, was to overcome my *lack of abundance*, money mindset barrier.

It was only after I changed my mindset, and believed that I could attract money in abundance through more than one way in life, that I became successful. Obviously, I also needed the tools and had to do the work to achieve the end result. Achieving a mindset of abundance allowed me to stay positive and approach obstacles with a *can-do attitude*.

Case Study

Rather than clog my mind with fear of failure and excuses as to why it may not work, I pushed through my previous mindset of lack, which I inherited from my upbringing, and moved into a mindset of abundance. This is a crucial piece to the entire formula for my success on Zazzle, and I would like you to objectively consider whether this is a crucial piece for you too.

I was coming from traditional 9 to 5 job experience, and had always worked trading hours for dollars. I had a mindset of *lack*, rather than *abundance*, because I could never see how I could achieve abundance with only so many hours in a day to do paid work. Also, my family taught me that the only way to become successful in life was to work hard, get a university education, and become a medical doctor. There were no other options in their minds. I do not fault them for their advice. It worked for many people, but it made me tired just thinking about it, and I did not want to keep trading hours for dollars, even though I would be paid more and be helping people, which I love to do.

Making money is important because you need enough to live comfortably, but it should not be the sole reason to get a particular kind of job that you dedicate your entire life to. You have to do what you love, and believe that the abundance will come. When you love doing a *job*, or something that earns you money, then you are good at it, you will experience abundance (monetary as well as spiritual). You will attract and create your own wealth doing what you were meant to be and do. If that means creating graphic designs, photography, or art, which you then sell on Zazzle to generate wealth, then you are in the right place at the right time.

The timing for making money on Zazzle is the best ever. Plus, you can use this book and my other resources to quickly get started and create abundance doing what you love.

The key is to have a mindset of abundance. Believing it is possible to receive money in abundance from Zazzle changes how you approach every aspect of what you do to set up, run, and grow your Zazzle business. Even if you have the tools and resources that will make it happen, a mindset of abundance allows you to be free to dream big and achieve beyond your wildest dreams.

This is proven over and over again in life, and also in my program. Every student has the same course material, live training, and mentoring, but some do better than others.

I can tell already who will succeed and who will struggle. Those who believe that Zazzle is the source of their abundance, and that they will receive in abundance if they implement my 5 Step Profit Plan strategy properly, exceed their earnings goals several times a year. They are not distracted by other people's lack of success on Zazzle. They go forth with confidence that there is abundance for them on Zazzle.

Money mindset barrier – Mistrust of method

This last money mindset I want to talk to you about is the most uncomfortable, but I have already helped many people through this *mistrust of method*, with positive results, so I think it is valuable for you to know about.

You may be completely convinced about everything I have written so far, and want to dive in and make oodles of money in the next year on Zazzle. Then you start The 5 Step Profit Plan Program™, you do the work, and time goes by and you don't make many sales. At this point, you look for a reason why things are not happening, and you instinctively begin to distrust the method. It makes sense as the perfectly logical place to look for blame. You can go down a really deep rabbit hole, thinking dark thoughts and playing the blame game, or you can realize it is a money mindset barrier that can sneak up on you unintentionally.

It makes perfect sense in your mind, and in the minds of others, that if you pay for training, you expect results. If you pay for a college or university education, you expect to get your degree, but you may actually fail and not graduate. If you graduate, you expect the best salaried job in your profession, but it does not always happen. You might say something like, "My degree from Harvard should open the doors to the top paying jobs." That may happen for some people, but it does not happen for every Harvard graduate. Then, if you don't receive that *best* job, you blame the degree, but not the actual reasons why you did not get the job: reasons that could range from the way you interacted with people during your interview, your university marks, your previous job history, your outside interests, or a better candidate.

It was not the degree and training, but what you put into it, what you got out of it, what you did with it, and that you believed it was the vehicle that would get you where you wanted to go.

This can also be said for my training. If you believe that The 5 Step Profit Plan™ is the roadmap that will take you on your journey to Zazzle success, then you will get the most out of it, do the most with it, and believe it will get you where you want to go.

The solution to this problem is reaching your first sale or first earnings target. Then your mindset instantly shifts to one of *trusting the method.* I did not give you more mentoring. You did not do more work. From one moment to the next, based solely on a result you have in your mind, your mindset automatically shifts. This happens a great deal with my clients that I am mentoring. It is only a matter of imprinting on your mind that the program works. Nothing else changes, but from then on, they are fired up, have expectations of abundance, and feel that they can accomplish anything.

You use your power to make this sudden mindset shift, based on reaching a goal or criteria that you arbitrarily set for yourself. That means you also have the power to make this mindset change before your goal or criteria is reached. You are in total control of whether or not you trust the method, and only you can put 100% faith behind it through your actions and attitude, and not use it as an excuse for lack of progress.

TAKE ACTION:
Write down in the "Notes," at the end of this chapter, what your money mindset barriers are after assessing your situation with brutal honesty.

No one will judge you. If you are truly honest, you will turn things around much more rapidly. Identifying the issue in any problem that is holding you back is the majority of the work. Second is accepting what you identified, and then it will be the least amount of work and effort to do something about it to improve.

Be good to yourself. Quiet introspection on your money mindset barriers, and finding ways to improve your mindset, will have a huge impact on your ability to generate wealth.

How to leverage your Zazzle income

Once you begin to make money on Zazzle, it's time to make decisions on how this money will be used. You will also want to leverage the earnings as a motivator to spur on your willingness to take massive action, and use it as a way to strategically increase your revenue. Let's dive into all of these 3 aspects in more detail.

Your Zazzle income is company revenue, not a personal salary

"Businesses must invest in products and people in order to create new wealth." – John Hoeven

First and foremost, your Zazzle income must be viewed as revenue for your company, not as a salary for you to pay your rent and expenses. Yes, at some point soon, you will want to receive money from your company in the form of a salary, and also enough additional money to put away to pay your income taxes. However, to start, you should consider re-investing your revenue from Zazzle back into your company.

To start, your monthly Zazzle revenue will be small and will only be paid out after the sale clears. I always assume I will be paid within 30 to 60 days of a sale, depending on when the items were sold, compared to when the monthly payout date is for Zazzle. Once the money is in your company's bank account (sole proprietor or LLC, or an incorporated company, etc.), invest in the company first before paying everything to yourself, to use for your own expenses. Use your Zazzle earnings to increase the assets of your company.

One asset type is your Zazzle store inventory. Use your Zazzle earnings to invest in ways that can help you make more products to sell. Purchase a commercial license to use a graphic design in new products you post or purchase. Place holder photos to improve the look of your template products on Zazzle. These and other investments will improve your inventory and increase your Zazzle store's ability to generate more revenue.

The tools that you work with on your Zazzle business are another type of company asset. You can improve the hardware and software you use to run your business. Purchasing a graphic design program or a new laptop are ways to increase your efficiency and ability to create more sellable designs.

"Invest three percent of your income in yourself (self-development) in order to guarantee your future." – Brian Tracy

The third asset is you. You are the company, and the only employee for the moment. You are the creative genius, the business expert, and the jack of all trades. Your business will only be as profitable as you are capable. That means you must always invest in yourself as you grow your company. At first, your investment might not have a monetary cost. Instead, it might be a time investment, like devoting time. You can watch *how-to* tutorials online, on whatever you need help with, to create Zazzle products that sell, and a profitable business. Then, once you have more funds coming in, you can pay for training courses, and finally get a coach and mentor to build your business to the 5, 6, and 7-figure level.

You may also be an investor in your own company. Use your personal money to invest in design elements, software, hardware, and personal training, instead of waiting until you earn enough on Zazzle. It is to your advantage to be equipped properly for maximum productivity. Also, the proper training can help you take proven action steps toward achieving your Zazzle earnings goal sooner. This will shorten the learning curve, and get sales to happen quicker than if you had done it all on your own.

TAKE ACTION:

Write down in the "Notes," at the end of this chapter, what portion of each Zazzle payout you will put toward investing in new product development, upgrading equipment, and personal development, in addition to the amount you take as a salary. The choice is up to you, and it may vary, payout to payout, but the main objective is to re-invest in your business and yourself, to help grow your business.

Use your Zazzle income as a motivator

The success of your Zazzle business depends on steady revenue coming in, and reaching a certain target by a certain date. You will have successes as well as failures on your Zazzle journey, as is the case with any business. The way to leverage your Zazzle income is to use it as a motivator to help you overcome the obstacles, and turn the failures into opportunities.

The most simplistic way to do this is to have an attitude of gratitude. Whether you made 29 cents like I did on my first sale, or you made $1,000 from one customer, you made a sale. You now have more money than you did before, and there is always the potential to make more.

If you can use that as a motivator, like I did, then you can overcome any obstacle, setback, or failure.

Case Study

Making and selling my first product on Zazzle—a button with polar bears on it—was easy, and it happened soon after I posted it for sale. I earned 29 cents from this button, and I was happier than when I got my first big paycheck at my real job. Why? Because I had found a new way to make money—a way that suited my needs. I could make money from my art and photography. I could work from home, when I wanted, and I had no ceiling on how much I could make. I knew it was the beginning of a new future for me.

But then, over the next few months, sales only trickled in, and my family and friends kept asking me, "Did you sell anything else? How much did you make?" Every time they asked me, I got more and more depressed. I had this false impression that I would make money fast, even though I had no idea what I was doing, and had no proven plan to follow to make it happen.

Now that I had not met my expectation, I was getting discouraged and embarrassed every time I was asked, "How are the sales?" I felt like I had put myself out there and told people about this new opportunity, and with every query, I had to defend my decision. The pressure on me to make sales created a negative situation that was harming me.

Then, one day, I realized that it was my own fault for letting other people get me down, and for allowing myself to think negatively about my progress. I was making money, just not the amount that I and others around me thought I should be making to consider it a success. I was putting this mindset on myself and not leveraging what I was accomplishing.

From that day forward, I decided to leverage my Zazzle income, no matter what amount it was, to help me succeed. I created an affirmation that I repeated to myself over and over again.

"If I can make 29 cents, then I can make more money on Zazzle."

I leveraged my first sale and made it an affirmation to succeed financially, and it worked! I made it a motivator rather than something that would discourage me. It worked for me because it reminded me that the hard part was over. I had found a way I could make money. All I had to do was find more products that would sell, and then things would multiply.

Over the years, this affirmation helped me as I grew my Zazzle business. To this day, I am grateful for each sale, large or small, that I make on Zazzle. Over time, those small sales got to be larger and larger yearly totals: first, it was 5-figures; then, 6-figures; and now, 7-figures yearly!

Yes, I am officially in the 2-comma club, and would never have been able to get there if I had lost hope or had gotten discouraged. I used my Zazzle earnings as a motivator daily, to keep taking massive action to achieve my financial goal. I continue to do this affirmation to this day. It always reminds me of what can be possible, as well as where I started.

Let your Zazzle earnings act as a motivator for your Zazzle journey to success.

TAKE ACTION:
Write down in the "Notes," at the end of this chapter, an affirmation that you can use to motivate you daily to take massive action and achieve your Zazzle earnings goal.

Use your Zazzle income to strategically increase your revenue.

Your Zazzle revenue is not just a lump sum of money you receive as a monthly payout. It is an incredible source of information about customer buying habits and sales data. Leveraging this information can increase your revenue stream exponentially, if you strategically build your product inventory based on your sales data. It may seem obvious, but you would be surprised at the number of Zazzle store owners who do not take advantage of this information. There are definitely barriers to obtaining the information, and time constraints on acting on it. However, even if you only take advantage of a percentage of the opportunities, your revenue will increase dramatically.

How this is done is too complex to explain properly in this book. There are many different things that need to be in place and that must all work together in order for you to leverage your sales data. That is why I created The 5 Step Profit Plan Program™ (https://elkeclarke.com/profit/).

You need all 5 steps implemented properly into your Zazzle business before it will be running effectively, and for you to be able to leverage your Zazzle sales data.

Your Zazzle business is a financial asset

Your Zazzle store (or stores) is your property, and it is a financial asset and investment. Your Zazzle business has a certain financial value currently, and it also has future value based on the current performance and future activity. It is important that you understand the full financial potential of your Zazzle business.

You own the images and designs that you have created and added to products that you posted for sale in your Zazzle store. They are your proprietary property, which can be used by you in any way.

You can profit from these images and designs in any other way you see fit. You can sell them on other print on demand sites, your own website, other types of online options, as well as in physical stores. You can sell them as digital products or physical products. You can license them to physical stores to sell on physical products. You can even get paid to have the Zazzle product with your design on it used in movies and TV shows as props on a set. The list is endless in terms of the revenue your designs can generate for your business, on Zazzle and off Zazzle.

Your Zazzle store is also an investment vehicle. It's like a dividend stock. Even if you don't do any work on your Zazzle store, it will still generate sales if you have good designs that are desired by customers. It can generate passive income for quite some time. The products posted are visible on Zazzle forever, if the product has sold at least once. If the product hasn't sold, it will be hidden after about a year. You can, at that point, edit it and set it as visible again. This means that you make a product once and it can sell for you many times, without you doing any more work.

I have products I made 10 years ago, and they still sell, year after year. It also means that a product can sell today for the first time, even though it has been sitting idle in your store for over a year. This makes Zazzle a fantastic place to invest the time to add product inventory, with the maximum chance of recurring sales for the longest period of time.

Imagine building your Zazzle store up over several years to generate over 1 million in sales every year, and then it continuing to sell similar amounts year after year, with little or no work. That would be amazing! Right? This is what happened to me. I built up my Zazzle business over several years, and then I began to enjoy the passive income that was generated while I enjoyed my free time.

You can also sell your Zazzle business. It is a lucrative opportunity for an investor, who would receive a good return on their investment, even if all they did was allow it to continue selling, and not add any more inventory. Plus, you can sell the rights to your copyrighted designs. There are many opportunities that you can take advantage of to profit from your efforts in creating a profitable online business using Zazzle.

Your Zazzle business is also your property to bequeath on the event of your death. This is important to remember and plan for in your estate planning.

Your Zazzle business is an extremely valuable commodity, and it is important to understand the full potential of how you can profit from it.

TAKE ACTION:
Write down in the "Notes," at the end of this chapter, how you will take advantage of your valuable asset once your Zazzle business is generating 6 and 7-figure a year revenue.

Elke's Secret to Success

Unblock your money mindset barriers to achieve financial success on Zazzle. Use your new Zazzle income wisely, and grow your financial asset.

Summary

In this chapter, I have helped you understand that your money beliefs play a big role in whether or not you will achieve your monetary goal. I have also provided you with ways that you can overcome your money blocks. In the next chapter, I will tell you what you need to know about creating your brand, and why it is crucial to your success.

Notes:

Chapter 9:

You Are Your Own Best Brand

"Customers don't just want to shop: they want to feel that the brand understands them." – Mickey Drexler

In today's world, customers are desensitized to traditional ways of marketing and advertising. They also are not as concerned about price and quality. Customers turn into buyers because they have an emotional connection with a brand. This makes it extremely important for you to develop and build your brand when you start your online Zazzle business.

I'm sure you have heard of brand loyalty. Loyalty originates from brands making customers feel like they are understood. Customers are also loyal to how a brand makes them feel. This is accomplished through the effect of the company's advertising and what the company represents. Effective advertising today does not focus as much on product quality and function, but rather on how the customer would feel if they used it, or what universal group they would feel as though they belonged to by using the product.

You, as a small business owner, can compete in this type of market by building your unique brand that will attract customers. In this chapter, I will show you several ways that you can build your brand and leverage your unique style and offerings in your Zazzle business.

Love what you do, and do what you love, to be successful

As an artist, photographer, and graphic designer, you have the ability to create your own unique designs. Your style will come through when you do what you love doing. This will result in truly unique designs and products, which only you can offer to the world.

When most people start out on Zazzle, they think that the only way they can make money is to *mimic* designs that are already bestsellers on Zazzle. This strategy backfires because of 2 reasons.

The first reason is that you are not offering anything different. When you continue to *chase* bestselling designs, then your Zazzle store's inventory will begin to look like a mish mash of various design styles. This clearly indicates that you are not offering anything new. As well, you never work on establishing your own design style and brand. It confuses your customers and does not create customer loyalty.

The second reason is that you are violating the copyright of other designers. This will result in legal issues and ultimate removal from Zazzle, which would be the end of your Zazzle business. The risk is not worth it.

It does not pay to copy. Create your own unique designs. Believe in yourself, and others will too.

Plus, if you love what you do, and do what you love, really well, then you will attract your own unique followers, because you have established your unique brand and design style that only you can offer.

Case Study

When I first started on Zazzle, I tried selling in various niches that I knew were popular. However, I did not have much success with them because I felt awkward designing for these niches. Once I started doing what I love, ideas flowed. I found a way to use my unique design skills to create desirable products for customers on Zazzle, in niches I loved working in. That is when people began recognizing my design brand and wanted to buy specifically from me as a designer.

To be successful, you must strive to achieve your unique design brand, or *secret sauce*, which will establish your unique identifiable brand.

Discover your "secret sauce" to establish your brand

Experiment with what sells on Zazzle. There are no costs to you to add products to your store, with various themes and designs. Try various things to find your combination of talents and what customers want. Zazzle is the perfect platform to do this because it is free to make as many different versions as you want until you find the right combination that sells. If you were creating physical products, you would not have this luxury and freedom to test the market, because each test would cost money.

Continue to post products with your unique designs on them. Your designs should be a marriage between your unique talents and what is currently trending, in order to create one-of-a-kind offerings that buyers want. Whatever this combination is that begins to create abundant sales for you, it will evolve into your *secret sauce*.

You won't recognize it right away, but soon you will make a comment: "So many of this one design is selling! This must be my secret sauce!" That's the non-scientific way of recognizing that you have found that sweet spot in your design brand.

Your *secret sauce* might be a design style, like minimal, floral, or vintage. For others, it might be a specific niche, like fashion or home décor. A third option is a unique combination of both, like a specific style within a specific niche. Once you recognize a trend among the designs and products that you are selling, you will be on your way to discovering what your *secret sauce* is, and how to use it to your advantage.

All the steps required to be in place to profit from your *secret sauce* is too complex to explain here. The 5 Step Profit Plan Program™, which I offer as my signature program, is specifically designed to help you build and profit from your unique brand.

YOUR ACTION STEP:
Write down in the "Notes," at the end of this chapter, what you think your secret sauce could be. What will define your uniqueness, which will also be the reason you will be successful on Zazzle?

Brand yourself through your design style to create more sales

At first, customers may buy your product without knowing that you are the designer. This happens because you had the design or product that the customer found online, which fulfills the need of that customer. It could have been a pillow that matched the color of their living room, with an abstract design on it.

At this point in the buying cycle, the customer is just happy that they found a blue and green abstract painting design on a pillow. However, after this first set of steps of finding the item and looking at it on the Zazzle product page, the opportunity to win the customer over with your design brand begins.

The customer may buy additional products that all have a similar design style, because the customer recognizes them as yours. The customer may also seek your products out because of your unique design style. Either way, you win, and you improve your sales, if you have unique products that have your branded design style.

Believe in your creativity and that your story has value

You can continue to earn money selling through the one-off strategy, where you have to attract each customer in some way, to buy for the first time from you. This can be effective and will grow your business to a certain level of success.

To achieve exponential growth, use your story to define your brand and grow your following. To get beyond selling a product only for its own value or purpose, get customers to buy your products just because of your brand.

Customers will buy brand name clothing for the sole reason that it is from a particular designer or has the name of the design house on it. This kind of brand buying loyalty is what you are striving for in your business. It will not happen overnight. It requires a combination of uniqueness on what you deliver and your story that customers resonate with. It could be something big, such as ending child poverty, or it could be less serious, like the fact that your posts on Instagram are fun and engaging.

Achieving brand frenzy is not a step-by-step process; more likely, it will be a random set of events that come together over time. The main components, however, consist of story-telling and offering unique items for sale that stand out so that people take notice.

The story-telling does not have to expose your personal life. If you are a photographer, you could be known as the nature photographer that takes photos of giraffes. Your stories would be all about what you do to save the giraffes in the wild, how you photograph them, the organizations you support with your philanthropy, and so on. If you are an artist, you can be *the pouring artist*, who creates dreamy abstracts by pouring paint onto canvases. Your stories would be all about your technique, involving people in choosing the colors for your next project, showing how you create the piece, and so on.

In both of these examples, your brand is being built through stories related to the production of your branded design style. The success of this strategy happens when you believe in your creativity and that your story has value.

Be consistent in your branding but constantly evolve

Once you create your brand, it is important to be consistent. If you are known for the abstract paintings you create as *the pouring artist*, then you cannot start showcasing realist paintings of dogs. Your current brand followers would be confused, and they would be disinterested in your switch because they love you for your abstracts.

However, let's say you switched from red and black abstract paintings to pastel shades of pink and blue abstracts, because that was the current color trend. This would be a good strategy for you to ensure that your brand stayed consistent as an abstract painter, but evolved with the times, in order that you continued to make sales.

Elke's Secret to Success

Only you can be you. Be authentic and relatable, and consistent with your brand; do what you love, and it will become your brand.

Summary

In this chapter, I introduced you to the importance of branding in the success of your Zazzle business. You can sell products based on providing a certain function or design, but to create exponential growth, you must build a brand. You can build your brand by being uniquely you.

Let your uniqueness come through in what you offer for sale, and in your story that you share, to involve your customers in the buying experience. In the next chapter, I give you the final piece to the puzzle of how you can make your dream a reality of making money online with your creativity.

Notes:

Chapter 10:

Live the Life of Your Dreams Doing What You Love

"If you can tune into your purpose and really align with it, setting goals so that your vision is an expression of that purpose, then life flows much more easily." – Jack Canfield

There comes a point in time in your life when you start to ask yourself deep and thoughtful questions about why you haven't achieved certain financial goals and personal goals on your bucket list. These goals keep hovering in the future as *"one of these days."* But why don't you feel that they are achievable now? Promise yourself that today is the day you change your mindset and take action to make the life of your dreams a reality.

What does your dream life look like?

Do you want...
- time and location freedom?
- financial freedom?
- creative freedom?
- the freedom to be and do what you love?

What makes you feel fulfilled in life? Why do you make certain decisions? Is it to make yourself happy? To support your family? We all have personal reasons, or a "why" in our lives. Your "why" will influence how you act, the choices you make, and the business risks you take, as well as your drive and commitment to succeed.

In Chapter 1 of this book, I talked about how most successful people claim that defining "why" was the key reason for their success. That is why I am going to dive in deeper on this topic here in my final chapter. I give you tools to help you create the life of your dreams.

First off, you have to become clear on what your "why" is. How you define your "why", or the driving force in life, will be uniquely your own. There is no right answer. No one will judge you. So be free, open, and honest with yourself when taking this journey of discovery.

To help you define your "why", answer these questions:

- What do you feel is the most important thing in your life?
- What makes your face light up when you talk about it?
- What reason makes you work longer hours than necessary, and push harder to achieve something, than you ever thought possible?
- If you are unhappy right now in your life, what change do you long for that would make you feel like you are living your dream life?

These are all actions that you take because of your "why".

Now that you have a better understanding of where your "why" originates from, it's time to define it.

Define your "Why" to live your dream life

Your "why" is what ultimately makes you happy. Your "why" can be defined as the ability to do or be in a certain state of action or being in your life. Our first instinct is to survive. You need to make enough money to be able to take care of yourself. You may be fortunate to already be in this position. Once we have taken care of surviving, we look for a meaning or purpose in our lives that drives us to do more, and experience more, beyond basic survival.

You want your life to be purposeful, meaningful, and filled with passion. You are seeking the experiences that will make you say: "I'm living my dream life!"

Your dream life might be a series of experiences that are on your bucket list, or they can be a core underlying state of being.

Let me give you some examples to help you define your "why".

Your "why" could be your family. Loving your family, protecting them, providing for them, and being the happiest you have ever been when you are with your family, all define that family is the center of your universe. You would do anything for them; you choose to help and be with them over other options you have. You would consider how something affects your family before you make choices in your life. Most of all, you feel it is your reason for being, and what you were put on this earth to do. This means that your family is your "why".

Your "why" is usually something personal rather than a dream job. The dream job is a means to achieving your "why". Your "why" could be to make the world a better place. Your dream job is a goal that fulfills your dream to make the world a better place.

You may think that your "why" is to make a lot of money, but it's most likely not true. Instead, your "why" is what you want to do with the money. With this money, you may want to be debt free, own your own home, and have enough money so that you don't have to work.

That means your "why" is to take care of you and your family. Or your "why" might be to stay at home and take care of a sick family member. Or it could be to spend time with your kids, and to experience those precious moments with them as they grow up.

Your "why" can also be a state of creative being. Being active in your passion can be your "why". As long as you are doing what you love, you will be happy. Your "why" would be defined as doing, or being in the state of doing, your passion daily. Some examples of this are designing, painting, doing photography, or other creative pursuits.

As long as you are doing it, no matter what you are making, producing, or earning from it, you are happy because you get to do it. This could also be related to family situations. If you love being a caregiver, then your "why" is being a mother, father, uncle, aunt, grandfather, or grandmother, etc. If you are a healer, you may be happy teaching yoga, running motivational retreats, or speaking on stage, but as long as you are healing lives, then that is your "why".

Case Study

For the first part of my life, I was living the "why" that my parents had defined for me—not my own "why". This makes sense because they were a big influence in shaping my life, and I had no reason to doubt my upbringing. I didn't even know that "why" could be defined, or that I had a choice to define it for me. I knew that I wanted to be successful like they wanted me to be, and I thought that I was doing things for me for the right reasons.

I thought I would be happy if I had a good education, a good professional job, and raised a family. As I began my journey to success, I realized that I had to define my own unique "why" to have the drive and motivation to achieve my dream goals and give purpose to my actions.

I was good at what I was doing, and really proud of all of my accomplishments in my professional job. I was in this job and chose this career because of the "why" that had been defined by my parents.

Being good at many things masked my true "why". I was living the life I thought would make me happy, but I was unhappy. I couldn't understand my unhappiness, and was embarrassed that I was unhappy, because others would love to have the life I had.

The true test came one day when the going got really tough. I was told I had to travel again for work, during a time that conflicted with an important family event. Even though my job was rewarding, and I was proud of what I accomplished, I did not have the commitment to have a career in the pharmaceutical industry. My "why" was my family and being creative.

Something had to change so that I would not burn out and continue to be unhappy.

That is why I quit my job and finally committed to being creative every day while being with my children. I was finally listening to my "why". With my "why" clearly defined, I set out to find ways to support my family with my creativity.

It was a struggle, but I was passionate and driven to succeed because, finally, my "why" was my true "why". It kept me determined to reach my goals despite any setbacks.

As time passes, your "why" will change or evolve.

Now that my children are grown, my "why" is still my family, but the focus has shifted more to me, my experiences, and how I can give to more than just my family. My "why" is to empower you, while exploring more of my creative abilities. This includes continuing to have the freedom to only work if I want to, when I want to, and where I want to. I am pleased to say that defining my "why" allowed me to focus on what is important to me, and gave me the strength to push onwards with a positive mindset to reach my goals.

I now have zero debt. My house is paid off. I paid for my kids' education. I have the time freedom to be with friends and family. I travel all over the world, for months at a time. Best of all, I continue to run and profit from my 7-figure Zazzle business.

Now it is your turn. What is your "why"?

TAKE ACTION:
In the "Notes" section, at the end of this chapter, write down your "why". What is your reason behind wanting to make money or to build your online business? It could be similar to some of the reasons I mentioned, but it can also be something totally different. Check in the Chapter 1 notes to see if what you now wrote matches what you wrote then. Your answer may have changed since Chapter 1, or maybe your "why" is now more clearly defined.

Escape the 9–5, have time freedom, and do what you love

Do you have a 9–5 job that you want to escape from, like I did? Do you want to prove to yourself that you can make money being creative, doing what you love? Do you want time freedom? Do you want to never have to waste time commuting to work ever again? Do you want to take off on vacation for several months of the year? Do you love that you can be with family and friends when important life events happen? What would you do if you were not restricted by your day job?

How would you feel if you could make money doing what you love? What would happen if your art, photography, and graphic designs, which you loved doing, would generate the wealth for you that you want and need to create your dream life?

Zazzle was my way to escape the 9–5 *(and still is, more than 10 years later)*, have time freedom, and do what I love. It also opened up so many doors for me that I did not know existed. Thank goodness I finally had the courage to define my "why," and decided to make my dream a reality.

Zazzle continues to be my income source. I have worked on my laptop from anywhere in the world that I travelled. Plus, I only work when I want to work.

I am passionate about what I do, and am joyful every day, because I can be creative and take care of me and my family from the income I receive from Zazzle.

Would you like this kind of freedom?

TAKE ACTION:
In the "Notes" section, at the end of this chapter, write down what your future will look like once you escape your 9–5 job (or any job or situation you have right now). What will you do with your time freedom? What exactly will you be doing that you love to do? Write out your typical day once you are working on Zazzle and growing your business. How will that make you

feel? Then write out your typical day once your Zazzle business is working for you creating passive income. How will that make you feel?

What do you need to make your dream life a reality?

To make your dream life happen, certain components must be working together to make it possible. Let's look at these and see how Zazzle easily facilitates each component.

"Financial freedom is freedom from fear." – Robert T. Kiyosaki

Financial Freedom: Freedom to earn the money you need, to do what you love

You will need **financial freedom** to live the lifestyle of your dreams. If your Zazzle business is set up properly, your Zazzle products can generate passive income for you while you are not working.

When I first started, I worked a lot of hours on Zazzle, but once I developed my 5 Step Profit Plan™, I built my business to 6-figures and 7-figures, working about 20 hours a week. Now, I only work a few hours a month to maintain my Zazzle business that generates over a million dollars in revenue yearly.

Some of my students who followed The 5 Step Profit Plan™ have built their Zazzle businesses from zero to 6-figures in revenue, in a little over a year. Zazzle is not a get-rich-quick income opportunity, but it pays off in the long run as your Zazzle products begin to sell over and over again, creating exponential growth and revenue.

The other thing I love about Zazzle is that there is no restriction on how much you can earn in a year. If you put in the work, you can generate all the wealth that you want. I like this much better, instead of working in a job where maybe, in a few years, if you overperform all the time and your boss likes you, you might get promoted to the next level of the pay scale. That is so limiting, and it affects how soon you can achieve even more time freedom.

When you have no restrictions on how much you can earn, you can decide how much extra effort to put into your Zazzle business to earn the amount of money you want. It's amazing what you can earn. With this Zazzle business model, you can achieve your lifetime income target sooner, and focus on the things that truly matter in your life.

Are you ready to get started?

Location: Freedom to work from where you want, doing what you love

You will need **location freedom** to be in the places you WANT to be, instead of where you HAVE to be, to generate an income. After quitting my job, one of the first glorious benefits was that I did not have to be in one restrictive cubicle in an office building.

I was so happy to no longer be with hundreds of anonymous people in their own little cubicles, all working on their computers, under neon lights, in a location that I had to spend 2 hours driving to every day.

I am so glad that I never again had to be at a job at a specific time, even if I had to risk my life driving in terrible weather conditions. The frustration was no longer there about having to take time off work to go to a medical appointment or take care of a family member that needed at-home care.

Over the years, companies and industries have definitely improved the quality of the working environment, with flex hours and working from home options. However, having the luxury of working for yourself and having complete control of when and where you work, while making the amount of money you want to make, certainly makes Zazzle a desirable option.

When you have no restrictions on where you can work, it's amazing what you can get accomplished. You can focus on the things that truly matter in your life.

Are you ready to get started?

Time: Freedom to work when you want, doing what you love

You will need **time freedom** to do what you love. When passive income is providing you with your income, you no longer have to trade your time for dollars. You can spend your waking hours creating more passive income opportunities, or doing what your time freedom affords you to do. Time freedom is the most precious commodity that there is.

Time freedom is liberating and eye opening. You will never look at free time in the same way. Instead of resting and recovering from your stressful, all-consuming (physically and mentally) demanding day job, you can fill your free time doing what you love. You will be able to feel joy, love, and passion, and live life every day, instead of surviving life.

Zazzle is the perfect option for you to obtain time freedom. If you set up your Zazzle business effectively, you can work less and earn more. You can work when you choose. You have the luxury of doing what you want in order to fulfill your "why," and then you can slip in your Zazzle work when it is convenient for you.

To this day, I find this to be the most glorious benefit. The time freedom my Zazzle business has given me has allowed me to travel on vacation for months at a time, take care of my loved ones 24/7 in times of need, pursue other personal goals on my bucket list, and now create training and programs to help you create a successful online business, all while still maintaining my 7-figure a year Zazzle business.

Isn't that fantastic? Would you like that kind of time freedom and financial freedom?

When your time is freed up, it's amazing what you can get accomplished. You can focus on the things that truly matter in your life.

Do you want to know how to easily get started?

How to live your dream life sooner

The most successful people credit their mentor, and sticking to a plan that works, as their reasons for achieving their success.

When you want to become the best at anything, you hire a mentor that is already successful at what you want to achieve. Why? Because you will decrease the time it takes you to achieve your goal.

Using a proven plan and successful mentor will give you the step-by-step roadmap to reach your goal, while providing you access to the years of experience of your mentor. These 2 components, combined, set you up for success that can be achieved much sooner than if you attempted to reach your goal on your own.

When I started on Zazzle, there was no one who publicly shared how to become successful on Zazzle. Even to this day, I am the only successful Zazzle designer who is publicly providing mentoring and training for you.

Since I had to figure everything out by myself, it took me much longer to achieve success on Zazzle. Do you have extra time to waste struggling and failing like I did? Or would you rather take advantage of my teaching and mentoring to achieve your financial goal on Zazzle sooner, so that you can live your dream life?

In this book, I have shown you how to:
- Define your "why"
- Set and achieve your dream goals
- Begin to develop the mindset of a successful entrepreneur
- Formulate an online business strategy to make money with your creativity
- Start your Zazzle journey to success

Your next step is to get the help you need to grow your Zazzle online business quickly, and with the least number of setbacks.

Would you invest in yourself and in your business, if you knew that you had found the easiest and best possible solution to accelerate the growth of your Zazzle business? My proven plan, The 5 Step Profit Plan™, and access to me as your Zazzle mentor, is the easiest and best possible solution for you. Plus, you can start today.

TAKE ACTION:
In the "Notes" section, at the back of this chapter, write out what things are standing in the way of you achieving your dream life. If you are already a designer on Zazzle, what is

missing from your skillset that has stopped you from already earning the level of income that you desire? If you are new to Zazzle, identify what you need, to achieve your earnings goal as soon as possible.

Now, answer honestly. Do you want to achieve your online income goal using Zazzle?

If you said "Yes!" with passion and determination, then answer this next question.

Can you achieve your goal on your own, or do you want help?

If you decided that you need help because you do not want to waste your valuable time, take action now and go to https://elkeclarke.com/profit/. Choose the training option that is best for you, and I will personally welcome you into the member's area, where you can get started right away.

I can't wait to guide you on your Zazzle journey to success, so that you can live your dream life sooner.

Elke's Secret to Success

Get started now! There is no time to lose, only precious time to gain.

Summary

In this chapter, I helped you define your "why," and gave you many reasons why Zazzle would be the perfect platform for you to use to achieve your dream of location freedom, time freedom, and financial freedom.

However, it's been my experience, and other's as well, that having a proven plan and a Zazzle mentor saves you time and improves your chances of success. That is why I am inviting you to join my signature 5 Step Profit Plan VIP Mentoring Program™. If you are committed to changing your life, and making your dream life a reality, using Zazzle, then I am equally committed to working with you as your mentor.

"The biggest adventure you can take is to live the life of your dreams." – Oprah Winfrey

Notes:

A Final Word

Congratulations! You're now ready to **create online and grow rich**.

I know that this book has helped you realize that you can become financially free using your creativity. If you felt frustrated that you had to compromise to earn your living doing something other than what you love, then this book has provided you with the solution. You now have the knowledge and power to achieve time freedom and financial freedom doing what you love.

I encourage you to keep this book handy and revisit it whenever you need a boost. My book's purpose is to be your guide, your inspiration, and your motivation on your journey to achieve your dream life. Look back at your notes that you wrote in this book to affirm your intentions to live your amazing, purposeful life. Finally, if you feel so inclined, please pass *Create Online and Grow Rich* on to any creative person in your life that you want to support.

With love and gratitude,

Elke

Resources

ELKE'S FREE BONUSES FOR YOU
To access Elke's free bonus cheat sheets, quizzes, and guides that are companions to this book, please go to
https://www.CreateOnlineAndGrowRich.com.

SOURCES OF COMMERCIAL FREE FONTS, PHOTOS, AND GRAPHICS
https://www.google.com/fonts
https://en.wikipedia.org/wiki/Wikipedia:Public_domain_image_resources
http://www.clker.com
https://pixabay.com
https://morguefile.com
The Zazzle Design Tool

Note: Always double check that the item you select from these public domain sites is truly free for commercial use.

FREE GRAPHIC DESIGN PROGRAMS
https://www.gimp.org
The Zazzle Design Tool

COPYRIGHT SEARCH TOOL – FOR THE UNITED STATES
https://www.uspto.gov/trademark

ELKE'S MOTIVATIONAL PRODUCTS

To purchase the affirmation and positive mindset products mentioned here in this book go to

https://www.zazzle.com/creativemillionaire

ELKE'S TRAINING - ZAZZLE ONLINE MARKETING AND BUSINESS STRATEGY

To obtain more information about The 5 Step Profit Plan Program™, and how you can enroll in the program, please go to https://elkeclarke.com/profit/

ELKE'S MENTORING RETREATS

To obtain more information about Elke's Mentoring Retreats and how you can transform you and your business through this amazing mentoring experience, go to

https://elkeclarke.com/premium-mentoring-retreats/

About the Book

This book takes you on a journey of self-discovery, empowerment, and transformation, while providing the system and processes for you to make money online using your creativity. Discover how to effectively monetize your graphic designs, photography, and art, using ecommerce and Elke Clarke's proven 5 Step Profit Plan™. In this book, Elke will inspire you, motivate you, and guide you on your journey to create online and grow rich.

About Elke Clarke

Elke is a 7-figure entrepreneur, international mentor, and success coach, who teaches online marketing and business strategies to digital creatives to build a profitable ecommerce business. Elke's signature 5 Step Profit Plan Program™ has helped entrepreneurs worldwide achieve their dream of owning a profitable online business.

Elke has been featured on Zazzle, Tough Nickle, Not So Niche, and Plus Your Business.

The authority on selling successfully on Zazzle, Elke is the author of her popular weekly blog at elkeclarke.com, and host of Elke TV, on YouTube.

Made in the USA
San Bernardino, CA
12 April 2019